D1549367

WITHDRAWN

Women
in Shakespeare

Women
in Shakespeare

Judith Cook

Harrap London

To
my father
who introduced me
to Shakespeare

First published in Great Britain 1980
by Harrap Limited
19-23 Ludgate Hill, London EC4M 7PD
Reprinted: 1985

© *Judith Cook* 1980

ISBN 0 245-53631-0

Designed by Robert Wheeler

Filmset by Woolaston Parker Ltd, Leicester
Printed and bound in Great Britain by
Billing & Sons Limited
Worcester

Contents

Illustrations

Preface

The idea of doing a book on the women's roles in Shakespeare's plays is one that has been at the back of my mind for a long time. But it was given a boost when in 1978 I suggested to *The Observer* that instead of doing an ordinary preliminary piece on the Royal Shakespeare Company's coming production of *Anthony and Cleopatra*, I should interview some of the actresses who had played Cleopatra over the years. What transpired was fascinating. All those I chose not only saw the character of Cleopatra differently, they actually produced the same quotes to prove totally opposite viewpoints. Cleopatra is the most complex of all Shakespeare's women's roles but many of the others are also open to a wide variety of ideas thanks to the genius of the writing—thankfully, there is no such thing as a definitive interpretation.

Having decided to look at these remarkable women, it was necessary to find some way of grouping them, which was an extremely difficult task. How you see the women is often very personal.

Back in 1832 Mrs Anna Jameson wrote a book on Shakespeare's heroines called *Characteristics of Shakespeare's Women— Moral, Poetical and Historical*, later to be reprinted several times under the simple name *Shakespeare's Heroines*. Mrs Jameson wrote prolifically on a wide variety of subjects from now unknown poets to books like *Social Life in Germany in 1840*. She was described as an 'indefatigable authoress' but the book for which she is now remembered is *Shakespeare's Heroines*. It is fascinating as a period piece. Much that she considered improper was censored out, even when the plot depended on it, but it does give a very good idea of how Shakespeare's female roles were viewed through the eyes of a woman of the mid-nineteenth century who seems to have been fairly typical of her time.

Mrs Jameson put her women into categories—'Characters of Intellect' included Portia, Beatrice, Rosalind, Isabella and Celia. 'Characters of Passion and Imagination' took in Juliet, Helena

Ophelia; 'Characters of the Affections'—Hermione, Desdemona and Constance.

Later, Dame Ellen Terry in a series of lectures published in 1932 also attempted a logical division, although she rightly said 'Shakespeare's characters are too idiosyncratic to fit this or that mould.' She had two main groups: 'Triumphant Women'—Portia, Rosalind, Volumnia, Beatrice and the Merry Wives, 'Pathetic Women'—Viola, Juliet, Desdemona, Emilia, Cordelia, Imogen and Lady Macbeth.

Categorization is, in fact, very hard, and I have done the best I can. Some group themselves neatly—the historical women (Roman and British), the earthy women like Mistress Quickly, the young tragic heroines. Others have obvious similarities—Viola and Rosalind, for example, and the outspoken females like Kate, Beatrice and Rosalind. Isabella and Portia I have covered in one chapter although their only similarity is that both are involved in a plot which hinges on their pleading for a man's life. More difficult is what one might term the 'suffering' women—Hermione, Imogen—and to them I have added Gertrude, as she is one of Shakespeare's few really passive women. In general chapters I look at the subsidiary female roles and the villainesses. Lady Macbeth and Cleopatra I felt to be so complex that they demanded solus chapters.

To throw as much light as possible on the characters, I have gone to a wide variety of sources, commentators both historical and theatrical, a look at the critics' viewpoints in the cases of Lady Macbeth and Cleopatra, and to actresses who have played many of them. We are fortunate in that Mrs Siddons left behind notes of performances, in particular a very detailed description of how she tackled Lady Macbeth.

A hundred years later Ellen Terry was tackling the same roles and she also left her views behind. Her nephew, Sir John Gielgud, says of her in his recent autobiography that 'she achieved the most perfect phrasing when speaking Shakespeare, a kind of frankness which made it seem as if she had just been taught the passage in the next room by Shakespeare himself'.

Moving to our own time, I went to actresses who have made a considerable reputation in a number of the roles and who can also

stand outside and discuss them objectively—Dame Peggy
Ashcroft, Judi Dench, Barbara Jefford, Jane Lapotaire and Janet
Suzman. In looking at Desdemona and Ophelia, I went to a
relative newcomer, Suzanne Bertish, for a young actress's view of these
two roles.

In general I have assumed that the plots of the most popular
plays are well known, and have only described at length those
which are less usually performed, such as *Pericles* and *The Winter's
Tale*. The first time a play is mentioned in detail I give source and
plot and date—although the latter is a matter of controversy
between scholars in many cases. I have taken the most common
datings.

There could, of course, be whole books written about almost
any of the individual characters; my scope was to look at the range
of them. No doubt there are mountains of source materials I should
have read but the size of this task falls into perspective when you
discover there have been some two hundred books written about
Measure for Measure alone. . . . I hope the book might help readers
understand a little more about the women described by A. L.
Rowse as 'the most marvellous gallery of female characters in
literature'. I can only say it has been a complete joy to write and
nobody could fail to be enriched who has spent months working
from those marvellous texts—marvellous in the true sense of the
word. It is the only writing project which I have not wanted to
finish.

Before coming to the acknowledgments, I would mention that
when working from the texts I have used the Arden editions of the
plays, published by Methuen, which are generally considered to be
excellent. The dating of Shakespeare's plays and the controversies
surrounding these would make whole volumes in themselves,
which is why it is necessary to say 'about' and 'it is generally
accepted' when giving a putative date. I had, however, to make a
decision on the overall pattern of dating, and I have chosen the
Arden dates as seeming the most likely.

I should like to thank the staff of the Shakespeare Centre in
Stratford for their help and the use of their facilities, the
Shakespeare Institute and the Royal Shakespeare Company. My
grateful thanks go to Mr Victor Bonham Carter for his special

help, and to the actresses who were prepared to give time and thought to help with the project.

Some of the material in the chapter on Cleopatra was previously published in *The Observer*, and is reprinted by permission.

My thanks are due also to Methuen and Co., Ltd, for permission to quote from *Shakespeare Our Contemporary* by Jan Kott; J. M. Dent and Sons for permission to quote from *Shakespeare, The Man and his Achievement* by Robert Speaight; and Macmillan, London and Basingstoke, for permission to quote from *William Shakespeare* by A. L. Rowse and *The Living World of Shakespeare* by John Wain.

The illustrations are reproduced by kind permission of the Shakespeare Centre, with the following exceptions: Vanessa Redgrave as Rosalind, Janet Suzman as Katharina, and Judi Dench as Beatrice (Holte Photographics Ltd); Judi Dench as Viola, Jane Lapotaire as Rosaline, and Judi Dench as Lady Macbeth (Joe Cocks); Judi Dench as Hermione, Janet Suzman as Cleopatra, and Glenda Jackson as Cleopatra (Reg Wilson); Fanny Kemble as Juliet (Mander and Mitchenson).

'Her infinite variety . . .'

The women in Shakespeare's plays range in age from the very young girls, like Juliet and Miranda, through the young women of the late teens and early twenties, to the full maturity of Lady Macbeth and Cleopatra. One of their most striking qualities is their independence. With rare exceptions, like Ophelia, girls defy their families and marry for love, disguise themselves as boys and follow their hearts, play a decisive part in determining their own fate.

Although his heroines tend towards an ideal, Shakespeare was writing as a man of his time. If the position of women in Tudor and early Jacobean England was scarcely enviable by today's standards, their influence was very considerable indeed and in general their lot had improved dramatically during the course of the sixteenth century. Educational opportunities—though mainly, of course, for wealthy women—had flowered, and although this still did not mean that girls were educated much outside their homes like their brothers, it did mean that they were offered considerably more than the ABC and texts of the old hornbooks. That some girls did go to schools of sorts can be gathered when Helena, in *A Midsummer Night's Dream*, searching for insults to use against her erstwhile friend Hermia, says that she was a vixen when 'she went to school'.

A woman who was an early notable scholar of the sixteenth century was Margaret Roper, daughter of Sir Thomas More, who had been tutored by him. He taught her Latin and Greek and philosophy, and as a young girl she sat at the feet of one of Europe's most progressive thinkers, Erasmus.

As early as the beginning of the sixteenth century, Erasmus had written a Colloquy between an Abbot (Antronius) and a learned woman (Magdala), contrasting the views of the conservative male of the day with those of the progressive female.

Antronius starts off with what we would call a typically male chauvinist statement: 'It isn't feminine to be intellectual: women are made for pleasure.' Magdala counters this by saying that she probably takes more pleasure in reading a good author than he does in hunting, drinking or gaming, so would he not consider her life to be a pleasurable one? Women's business, continues Antronius, is the affairs of her family and the instruction of her children. Here Magdala's response leaps the centuries to our own day. Yes, she says, indeed it is so important that it takes much wisdom to do it. So the more wisdom that can be gained through books and learning, the better.

'Books destroy women's brains who have little enough themselves', continues Antronius, obviously feeling he is not doing too well. 'Bookishness makes folk mad, by my faith, I would not have a learned wife. I have often heard it said that a wise woman is twice a fool.' 'A woman that is truly wise does not think herself so; but on the contrary, one that knows nothing thinks herself to be wise and that is being twice a fool.' Which seems to give game, set and match to Magdala.

Martin Luther, writing in 1531, also epitomized the conservative outlook. 'Women ought to stay home; the way they were created indicates this, for they have broad hips and a wide fundament to sit upon, keep house and bear and raise children.'

But as time went by, especially in more progressive circles, such advice was not heeded. Indeed, Queen Elizabeth herself arrived in her teens able to speak half a dozen languages, and at the age of twelve had painstakingly translated a 128-page religious poem from the French of Marguerite of Navarre. She could also write music and play the virginals prettily, and even her worst enemies had to admire her learning and intellect. That she also had a practical bent was shown by her flat refusal (at the age of six) to give her baby brother Edward any of the suitable gifts of gold and jewellery offered to her for the purpose. She said she would make him a cambric shirt, and she did. Elizabeth's tutors had been first,

William Grindal, a progressive who condemned the flogging of children to make them learn, and Grindal's own master, Roger Ascham. Between them they taught the young Elizabeth French, Italian, Flemish, Spanish, Greek and Latin, along with history, geography, mathematics, astronomy and the elements of architecture.

An equal scholar was Elizabeth's cousin, Lady Jane Grey, whose tragic death at the age of sixteen destroyed a bright promise. From the age of four she had been taught Greek and Latin by her tutor, John Aylmer, who was to record that hers was the brightest mind with which he had ever come into contact.

During Shakespeare's own time the great ladies of the noble families, the Cecils and the Sidneys for example, were renowned for their scholarship, but we know less about the educational opportunities of the women in the kind of society from which Shakespeare himself came. It is significant that when he portrays them in his plays they are very definitely literate and numerate. Maria in *Twelfth Night* can forge her mistress's handwriting well enough to convince even the lady's own steward that it is truly that of Olivia, and on that ability hinges the comedy plot of the play. The ladies in *The Merry Wives of Windsor*, the merchants' wives Shakespeare must have known so well, can laugh or fume over a clumsily turned phrase in the letters each one has received from Sir John Falstaff.

How much of the women in his own life Shakespeare put into his plays is a question about which argument is unlikely to cease. Not very much is known about his wife, Anne, except that he was rushed to the altar to ensure the legitimate birth of his first child, and that eighteen months later she presented him with twins. She survived him by seven years, and he left her his second-best bed.

Shaw, in a satirical essay called *A Dressing Room Secret*, has Shakespeare say some scathing things about poor Anne. 'I meant Lady Macbeth to be really awful; but she turned into my wife . . . if you notice, Lady Macbeth has only one consistent characteristic, which is, that she thinks everything her husband does is wrong and that she could do it better.'

Some commentators note a change in Shakespeare's attitude to his women characters which begins with Juliet. Dame Ellen Terry puts it down to a love affair, and says confidently that the lady was Mary Fitton, 'the Dark Lady of the Sonnets'. That the Dark Lady had a tremendous influence on him no one will argue, but it is unlikely that she was Mary Fitton, one reason being that Mary Fitton was blonde.

A. L. Rowse plumps for Emilia Lanier as the Dark Lady. She was certainly very dark, came of a musical family, lived on the fringes of both Court and theatrical society and was married, but promiscuous. He makes out a convincing case for this lady, whose husband was also called Will, and feels Shakespeare was getting at this in the lines

> Whoever hath her wish, thou hast thy *Will*,
> And *Will* to boot, and *Will* in overplus.

The word 'will' is a bawdy Elizabethan pun, moreover, but whoever she was there are possible traces of her in Rosaline and in Beatrice.

There is also a theory that Shakespeare had a child by the wife of an Oxford vintner, John Davenant. His wife was said to be well read and a very beautiful woman of 'a good wit and conversation extremely agreeable'. She was a woman of the playwright's own background, too. Certainly there was a child, William, to whom Shakespeare stood as godparent, and who later became a poet in his own right—in fact, Poet Laureate. He would never either confirm or deny his paternity; which is hardly surprising. We are indebted to John Aubrey as one source of this story, writing only a generation later and as an acquaintance of William D'Avenant. Aubrey observes on the matter: 'Sir William would sometimes when he was pleasant over a glass of wine with his most intimate friends say that it seemed to him that he writt with the very spirit that Shakespeare did, and seemed content enough to be thought his son.'

One certainty is that Shakespeare was extremely fond of his daughters, Susannah and Judith, and possibly the young and lovely girls like Perdita and Juliet have overtones of his own.

When you read accounts of the time you feel that life had a tremendous sense of pace and urgency. For so many Elizabethans life was very short: plague, smallpox and cholera, among other things, saw to that. Shakespeare's own family was far from untypical, for his brothers died in their twenties and thirties, a sister at the age of eight and his own son at the age of eleven. His descendants died out with his grandchildren, none of whom reached thirty.

So marriage came early to most women, as, indeed, did childbed. It is not only today's teenagers who mature early. 'Younger than she are happy mothers made', says Paris, pressing old Capulet to let him marry the barely fourteen-year-old Juliet. Indeed, Juliet's mother echoes this, saying that many ladies of esteem in Verona

> Are made already mothers, by my count
> I was your mother much upon these years
> That you are now a maid.

For most women there followed prolonged years of child-bearing, and that so many managed to keep their health, strength and wit says much for their stamina.

Commentators of the day, like Thomas Platter, writing in 1599, said that 'England is a woman's paradise, a servant's prison and a horse's Hell', while the misogynist Philip Stubbes said in his *Anatomie of Abuses* in 1583 'there are some sober, wise, gentle and descrete and vertuous matrons, as may be in all the worlde. And there be othersome (yea, more numerous) that are never well but when they be eyther brawling, scolding, or fighting with some of their household and such devils as man were better to be hanged than dwell with them.'

That women enjoyed the theatre was shown by an anonymous contemporary source. 'In our assemblies at plays in London you shall see such heaving and shoving, such itching and shouldering to sit by the women, such care for their garments that they be not trod on—such pillows for their backs that they take no hurt, such giving them pippins to pass the time, such playing of footsaunt without cards, such tickling, such toying, such smiling, such winking and such manning them home when the sports are ended.' Footsaunt or cent-foot was apparently a game of cards where the terms used in the game also had to do with love.

So Shakespeare reflected the women of his age, the witty learned ladies, the independent wives, even the rural simpletons— no doubt he came across many an Audrey on market days in Stratford, especially at the October Mop, Stratford's great hiring fair (which still takes place today, although its origins are largely forgotten).

On stage, women in Shakespeare's day were, of course, portrayed by boys. It is an interesting fact that we know the names of many of those who created the great sixteenth-century male roles. We know that Edward Alleyn played Tamburlaine and Faustus, and that Richard Burbage created Hamlet and King Lear. We know the great clowns like Kempe and Arnim (or Armin): the former appears in the cast list as Dogberry, the latter created Feste and the Fool in *Lear*. Tradition has it that Shakespeare played the Ghost in *Hamlet* and Adam in *As You Like It*. The latter source is an old Stratford neighbour who when asked for his recollections of the poet remembered he had seen him in that role 'brought on the stage on another man's back'. (Shakespeare's brother Gilbert seems also to have remembered this.) But the names of the boys who played Shakespeare's girls and women do not appear in any of the contemporary cast lists.

A handful of names of boy actors survive. Maybe the reason more did not come down to us through the centuries is that their professional careers were of necessity brief. Colin MacInnes put forward this theory in a novel about Shakespeare's life, and it gave the book its title, *Three Years to Play*—the years from thirteen to sixteen, when these boys created the female roles in sixteenth and early seventeenth century drama.

One name that has come down to us is that of Nathan Field, who was a rarity in that he successfully transferred from girls' roles to those of leading men. He was born in 1587, so his career overlapped that of Shakespeare, and his name appears in cast lists for the plays of Jonson. It also appears as seventeenth on a list of twenty-six boy players in the First Folio as a member of Shakespeare's company, but we have no proof that he played in Shakespeare. He later went on to become a playwright himself.

A name immortalized for us by Jonson is that of Salomon Pavy. Jonson has left an epitaph for him, in which occur the lines

> Years he number'd scarce thirteen ...
> And did act, what now we moan
> Old men so duly.

Boy players could be apprenticed to the theatre as to any other trade, and we know that there was a boy called James Sands, apprenticed to Augustine Phillips of Shakespeare's company. Phillips left him forty shillings and some musical instruments in his will, and that the boy was gifted and popular was shown by another bequest, this time of £40 in the will of William Sly, an actor in the same company, who died in 1608. Forty pounds was a considerable sum for that period: Shakespeare paid only £60 for New Place. We do not know if he played girls' roles, but as he was a musician he no doubt sung Shakespeare's songs. There is, one supposes, a possibility that Shakespeare's own brother, Edmund, may have played some of the parts. He joined the company when he was very young, and died at the age of twenty-seven, shortly after his bastard baby son.

In the Lord Chamberlain's Company (later the King's) for which Shakespeare wrote there must have been two good boy actors over a period of time, one short and one tall. They would portray Viola and Olivia, Celia and Rosalind, and reference is made again to their disparity in height in the quarrel scene from *A Midsummer Night's Dream* when Helena calls Hermia a dwarf and Hermia replies by describing her friend as a 'painted maypole'.

But how boys in general were able to tackle the complexities of women's roles at that time remains a mystery. Peter Quennell says that it probably worked out well enough in the roles written for the very young women, but he was doubtful about the mature roles. Certainly the breeches parts suited the custom of the time, for as well as making the portrayal of those girls even easier, plots in which girls appeared in travesty as boys were immensely popular with Elizabethan audiences.

Says Quennell, 'With their strange mixture of innocence and experience, romantic feeling and sharp spoken candour, masculine bravado and feminine nervosity, they tread a delicate line between the sexes. None of them is a completely mature woman; they belong to a period of human existence when the mildest girl is sometimes tomboyish and even the most energetic boys may now and then shed girlish tears. They are impetuous, high-spirited, naturally provocative and, at times, aggressive.'

A. L. Rowse, on the same subject, says that in the masculine world of the theatre in which Shakespeare was so wholly engaged, he would not have had a wide variety of womenfolk in view . . . 'and he would have had to keep in view the capacities of the boy actors to act the parts. One can easily see boy actors in the parts of Rosaline, Beatrice, Rosalind or Portia; or as Calpurnia, Constance or Hotspur's wife; or Ophelia, Desdemona, Imogen, Miranda. One has known boys who would do very well as Cressida. But what about Lady Macbeth and Cleopatra? One can only suppose that the emotional and intuitive potentialities of youths were more fully realised by the Elizabethans.'

Perhaps it was that very complexity of the mature women's roles which is the reason why there is no record of *Antony and Cleopatra* being played in Shakespeare's own lifetime, and why *Macbeth* received relatively few performances. Actress Janet Suzman puts forward an interesting theory when discussing Cleopatra that perhaps there was an astounding drag actor in the company who could manage such roles. But if there was, then there is no record of him.

Possibly Shakespeare realized that he was writing for well outside his own time. In a recent essay, art critic John Berger postulated a theory on painting which could as well apply to writing of genius. He said that photography provided only an accurate record of the past, it recorded a frozen instant in time, but great painting was far more than a record: it was also a prophecy. 'Paintings are prophecies received from the past, prophecies about what the spectator is seeing in front of the painting at that moment.' Surely the same can be said of Cleopatra?

But before we examine in detail Shakespeare's female roles, it is interesting to look at the parts for women in plays by a few of his contemporaries. Probably the earliest women with any personality at all appeared in the mystery plays, such as Noah's wife in the Chester Cycle. In the earlier part of the sixteenth century there was the young girl in Udall's *Ralph Roister Doister*, which was

written some time between 1552 and 1567, and the women in
Gammer Gurton's Needle, an anonymous play which was probably
somewhat earlier. Slight but delicious female parts occur in some
of Shakespeare's immediate predecessors, as in Lyly's *Campaspe*
(1584). Indeed, the *Cambridge History of English Literature* remarks of
Lyly that he was 'the first to bring together on the English stage
the elements of high comedy'.

Although a fairly wide range of women appear in the body of
sixteenth and early seventeenth century plays whose texts still
exist, no other single writer produced anything like the variety of
female roles. Interestingly, Shakespeare's two great contemporaries, Christopher Marlowe and Ben Jonson, did not serve
women too well—the first perhaps not surprisingly, given the
nature of his sexual tastes, the second because he does not seem to
have rated women particularly highly himself. (Perhaps, though,
it might be pointed out here that Nathan Field, already mentioned,
created the role of Epicoene in *Epicoene, or the Silent Woman* in 1969.)

In Beaumont and Fletcher's play *Philaster*, first played about
1608, we have a heroine who disguises herself as a boy. Euphrasia,
daughter of the villainous Dion, does this in part to be able to
follow the hero, Philaster, whom she loves. He seems little
deserving of such devotion; a shallow youth, who stumbles from
one misadventure to the next.

In strength of affection Euphrasia probably matches Viola,
although she is not given such rare verse to speak. She is also
something of a doormat, and repeatedly says that she is too low-
born for Philaster. When her disguise is revealed she says to him

> . . . sitting by window,
> Printing my thoughts in lawn, I saw a God,
> I thought (but it was you), enter our gates:
> My blood flew out and back again, as fast
> As I had puffed it forth and sucked it in
> Like breath. Then was I called away in haste
> To entertain you. Never was a man,
> Heaved from a sheep-cote to a sceptry, raised so high
> In thoughts as I: you left a kiss
> Upon these lips then, which I mean to keep
> From you forever.

Unlike Viola, that is all she does keep, for Philaster loves another, and so Euphrasia settles for a spaniel-like devotion and the privilege of being able to wait on them both hand and foot for the rest of their married lives. She does indeed end up in the equivalent of Viola's willow cabin in *Twelfth Night*, and nowhere does she show the spirit of a Viola or a Rosalind.

A far livelier lady appears in another Beaumont and Fletcher— or Beaumont—play, *The Knight of the Burning Pestle*, published in 1613. The Citizen's Wife would make a fit companion, one feels, for Mistress Quickly or Juliet's Nurse. You could imagine them at the theatre together. Having persuaded the players to take on her own apprentice, Ralph, in a leading role, she then climbs on to the stage from time to time to make a few points. When seated in the audience she addresses her long-suffering husband, her neighbours and her apprentice, in his translation to the role of a Thespian. She is only slightly larger than life, and we have all sat in front of her equivalent in theatres and cinemas today. Another group of energetic ladies appear in Thomas Dekker's *The Shoemakers' Holiday*, first published in 1600.

But many of the women who figure in the late Elizabethan or Jacobean plays appear in the so-called Revenge tragedies, those plays which T. S. Eliot describes as showing 'the skull beneath the skin'. They can be either suffering victims or outright villainesses. Castiza, in Tourneur's *The Revenger's Tragedy*, published in 1607, is indeed the embodiment of chastity and a pawn used by her brother, Vendice, in his evil plotting; but she remains two-dimensional.

Far, far more rounded is the Duchess of Malfi, 'the Duchess without a name', as Janet Suzman describes her, in Webster's play of that name, which was first published in 1623 but was most likely played in 1612. Having defied her family and married her own steward, she is the victim of a prolonged vendetta at the hands of her family, especially her brother, who obviously betrays some kind of incestuous passion for her. Locked away among the insane, she keeps her sanity, and is finally murdered about two-thirds of the way through the plot.

Janet Suzman says that her tragedy was 'that she wanted to be terribly ordinary, have domestic warmth, babies, a man to love—it was as simple as that—but she gets involved in a terrible duplicity and so lies. When she loses her integrity she pays the worst consequences. It was amazing that Webster should see such a woman and recognize her needs and then set her in such a class-conscious structure.'

Her death scene provides her most memorable lines. 'I pray thee, look thou giv'st my little boy some syrup for his cold,' she pleads, movingly. When told she is about to die, and asked if she is terrified of the cord with which she is to be garrotted, she replies

> Not a whit:
> What would it pleasure me to have my throat cut
> With diamonds? or to be smothered
> With cassia? or to be shot to death with pearls?
> I know death hath ten thousand several doors
> For men to take their exits; and 'tis found
> They go on such strange geometrical hinges,
> You may open them both ways.

The mystery, says Janet Suzman, is why she is so willing to die. 'It was when I thought of this I saw the similarities with Cleopatra—they both embrace death—for both embrace it as a perfect choice. They wish to make an end. Death becomes a kind of lover. Webster gives his Duchess great dignity.'

Neither Vittoria in Webster's *The White Devil* (first published in 1612) nor Beatrice in Middleton's *The Changeling* (first published in 1653, but first licensed for performance in 1623), approach the grandeur of Lady Macbeth, although both are interesting in their different ways. Beatrice seems curiously contemporary, a heroine out of a twentieth-century psychological drama.

Vittoria never really pretends to be other than ruthless. As the play proceeds she shows herself to be an adulteress who connives at the murder of her own husband, and who marries a lover who has himself murdered his first wife. She is prepared to go to most lengths to have her own way. The guilty pair are pursued by the families of both dead partners and Vittoria is finally brought to trial before a court that she does not hesitate to point out is rigged against her.

She is fiercely independent and outspoken and very much her own woman, and when she dies, like some of Shakespeare's villains—notably Richard III and Macbeth—she shows real courage. Stabbed by her murderer, she says

> 'Twas a manly blow!
> The next thou giv'st, murder some sucking infant;
> And then thou wilt be famous.

She ends, pathetically,

> My soul, like to a ship in a black storm,
> Is driven, I know not whither.

and her brother Flamineo advises 'Then cast anchor.'

Beatrice is an even more remarkable creation. At the outset of the play we see her as she sees herself, a dutiful daughter going along with her family's plans to marry her to Alonzo, although she is actually in love with Alsemero. But there is obviously something already deep inside her which responds all too readily to the suggestion of De Flores, one of her father's gentlemen, that he is quite willing to murder Alonzo for her so that she can marry Alsemero.

She spends much time telling us how repellent, loathsome and evil she finds De Flores—so much so that it appears even at this stage that he holds a tremendous fascination for her. His price for the murder is her virtue, and she rashly promises it, thinking that when the time comes she will be able to talk herself out of the bargain; but she has reckoned without the ruthlessness of De Flores.

There are some high comedy scenes, such as her successful accomplishment of the tests set by her suspicious husband to prove she is a virgin bride, and a strange sub-plot. The Changeling of the title is her servant girl, with whom she works the 'bed switch' trick also used by Shakespeare in *Measure for Measure* and *All's Well That Ends Well*. Unhappily, she murders her poor servant girl to shut her mouth.

Gradually, step by step, Beatrice is drawn into ever more deceit, indeed into further murders. Painfully she learns that she cannot use any means to achieve any end and yet remain unsullied, that she cannot violate all the laws of humanity and morality and escape the consequences of what she has done. Her progress throughout the play is a constant stripping away of layers of pretence, through to a terrible self-knowledge when she finally sees herself for what she is—a mirror image of De Flores himself.

It would be wrong, therefore, to say that only Shakespeare in his time created believable and fascinating roles for women. The difference lies in his ability to write convincingly and beautifully for so many different types of women. Rosalind and Viola are much finer characters than poor Euphrasia, Lady Macbeth shows us a more divided soul than Vittoria. Perhaps only Middleton's Beatrice rivals Shakespeare's women in her complexity, but she nowhere achieves the range of Cleopatra.

'My father had a daughter lov'd a man . . .'

Rosalind and Viola are Shakespeare's truly golden girls, but before we look at them it is interesting to consider a character that in many ways foreshadows them—Julia in *The Two Gentlemen of Verona*. Julia too goes on a journey to a strange land disguised as a boy, and she also is used as an emissary by the man she loves in the court he pays to the woman of his choice. We have to accept in all three cases that the girls can completely fool their men into believing that they really are boys and accept that the men do not recognize them. (Not content with that, in two of these cases they go on to fool other women!) But having disguised themselves, all three girls react differently. Julia begins as an initiator of action and becomes a passive character waiting for things to come right; Rosalind is an initiator throughout, making things happen; Viola again is passive, waiting for time and fate to unravel the complicated knot in which she finds herself.

The Two Gentlemen of Verona is one of Shakespeare's earliest plays, but there are many doubts about the date. Its probable date is given as 1592/93. Unlike most of the other comedies, there is no definite source for the plot. Briefly, the story shows what happens to friendship when love—especially the wild infatuations of adolescence—intervenes. Proteus and Valentine have been close and intimate friends, a bond which is wearing thin as Proteus becomes involved with Julia. Valentine sets out to seek fame and fortune at the Court of the Duke of Milan, where he is followed by Proteus. The naive Valentine raves to Proteus about the wonders of his lady-love, Silvia, and confides that he is going to elope with her. Silvia is the Duke's daughter, and as soon as Proteus sees her he also falls madly in love with her and decides to ingratiate himself with her father by telling him of Valentine's plans.

Valentine is banished, Proteus is favoured and meanwhile poor Julia, having heard nothing from her lover, disguises herself as a boy and sets out to see what has happened to him. She finds out soon enough, and in her disguise is actually used by Proteus to send messages to Silvia (who admittedly gives him no encouragement). After many misunderstandings and adventures all comes right in the end, during which there is an extraordinary scene where Valentine not only forgives Proteus's treachery but offers him Silvia for good measure, irrespective of the feelings of either girl, such being the bond of friendship.

In a production by Robin Phillips at Stratford in 1971 the characters became students of a kind of Golden Age college with the Duke as its head. At the end the two couples were left looking thoughtfully at each other in a way that suggested they were still uncertain of the choice they had made. 'In love, who respects friend?', cries Proteus.

In this production Ian Richardson gave Proteus a kind of youthful Iachimo type of duplicity, but on the whole the leading roles in the play have little depth, with the exception of Julia. The beautiful Silvia, over whom all the fuss is about, remains cool and somewhat unsympathetic. In a commentary by M. C. Bradbrook, writing on *Shakespeare and Elizabethan Poetry*, she says of Silvia, 'it has been asked how she should be expected to react to the summary disposal of her favour. Clearly she should not react at all. She is the "prize" for the purpose of argument and must not call attention to herself . . . she is a lay figure. Leading ladies may not relish this but boys would have been more tractable.'

But Julia is genuinely in love, and we see it first in her comic reaction to the letter from Proteus. 'She goes off', says Miss Bradbrook, 'in disguise to look for a love whose fidelity she never doubts. We know already of the loss of that love which makes it poignant.'

So we watch Julia carried away by the excitement of her proposed journey and disguise, buoyed up by the enthusiasm she feels for the adventure on which she has set out and brimming with joy at the prospect of seeing Proteus again. The other characters—again perhaps foreshadowing others in *Twelfth Night*—seem more involved with the affectations of love, of the idea of being in love, while Julia's affections are very real. Julia, continues the commentator, has a 'wit that co-exists with, sets off, grows out of and deepens with her sadness'. She has taken on the life we associate with Shakespeare's later heroines. Anne Barton, writing of Julia in notes in the programme for the Phillips production, says: 'Julia perhaps comes closest of all the characters to achieving a synthesis of the play's polarities: realism and romanticism, mockery and faith, detachment and involvement, wit and passion'.

It is noticeable, too, that Julia and Silvia respect the idea of friendship as do later couples—Helena and Hermia, Beatrice and Hero and, of course, Rosalind and Celia. When the play ends we cannot but wonder if Julia will be happy with Proteus, if he will turn out to have been worth it. Silvia and Valentine raise no such problems, since their two-dimensional reality ceases with the end of the play.

Julia was an orphan, and Rosalind and Viola are motherless girls, which gives rise to an interesting point made by the actress Janet Suzman, who pointed out that of all Shakespeare's major heroines, in comedy or tragedy, only Juliet has a mother. The rest are motherless, and she wondered why this was. Many girls—Hermia, Celia, Ophelia, Kate, among others—are shown in relation to their fathers, but we never learn what the mother-daughter relationship was like. Was it, one wonders, a dramatic device to ensure that so many of the girls had such independence?

So we come to the Forest of Arden and *As You Like It*. As in the case of most of the comedies, there is again disagreement as to the date, but the majority opinion sets it in 1599, written immediately before *Twelfth Night*. One source puts it as far back as 1592, but this seems most unlikely in view of the maturity of the writing.

The source was undoubtedly Thomas Lodge's romance *Rosalynde*, a story he himself borrowed from a fourteenth-century source. Virtually all the characters used by Shakespeare appear in Lodge's high-pastoral drama, with two important and essential exceptions—Touchstone and Jaques. These are entirely Shakespeare's own creations. Lodge's original story had more melodrama—including bribes, kidnapping and threats of vengeance—but Rosalynde does indeed become Ganymede. However, Rosalind's famous cure for love which she tries on Orlando—knowing quite well it will have the reverse result—does not come into the original.

Rosalind is a part which offers an actress all the wit, liveliness and joy anyone could wish for. Of all Shakespeare's romantic heroines she is the most realistic. 'Men have died from time to time,' she tells Orlando, 'and worms have eaten them, but not for love.' But then she has complete faith in Orlando's love for her and all the security that brings, unlike her successor, Viola. Shakespeare never lets us forget that she remains, in spite of her disguise, very much a woman. 'Do you not know I am a woman? When I think, I must speak.'

As Helen Gardner said, in a lecture at a 1955 Shakespeare Summer School: 'If Rosalind, the princess, had attempted to cure her Orlando she might have succeeded. As Ganymede, playing Rosalind, she can try him to the limit in perfect safety, and discover that she cannot mock or flout him out of his "mad humour of love to a living humour of madness" . . . by playing with him in the disguise of a boy she discovers when she can play no more.' In the same sequence of lectures, John Wain says: 'The girl in boy's disguise uses the immunity of that disguise to instruct her lover in how she wishes to be approached. It is an elaborate sexual game, as solemn and intricate as the country dances of birds and insects.'

Like Viola later, Rosalind becomes the object of affection of a real woman, in her case the cool shepherdess Phebe. Rosalind reacts in anger: 'Sell where you can,' she tells her, 'you are not for all markets.' Phebe, having scorned the love and devotion of Corin, has been punished by Eros with a passion for Rosalind as sudden and overwhelming as that of Titania for Bottom, and becomes a thing of straw, loving 'at first sight'.

Agnes Latham in her introduction to the Arden edition of the play says: 'In Arden Rosalind finds her freedom. She is no longer living on sufferance at the usurper's court and in doublet and hose she is no longer confined to a woman's limited role.

'Her own temperament frees her from the restrictions of romantic love . . . this does not mean that she is in the least destructive of love itself or resentful of its compulsive tides in which she is happily drowning. What she will not countenance is an affected and humourless intensity, the besetting fault of Elizabethan love cults. Once in the forest it is she that takes control—even of her father, to whom she makes herself known in her own good time—and Shakespeare puts the dénouement into her capable hands. Without her earlier misfortunes she might seem almost too managing, but when we first meet her she is sad, so that it is a pleasure to watch her spirits bubble up. She comes into her own, and into a better heritage than she has lost.'

Like many of Shakespeare's plays, *As You Like It* received only pirated and travestied performances for long after his death, and the first revival with a text which approximated to the original was given in 1740 at Drury Lane with Mrs Pritchard as Rosalind. From 1741 to 1750 Mrs Pritchard and Mrs Woffington were rival Rosalinds, while the ubiquitous Mrs Yates took it on in 1761. Mrs Siddons tried it in 1785 and 1786, but was criticized for doing so, as she had become in the popular mind a tragedy queen. It would be fascinating to know how she portrayed it—possibly nearer in style to interpretations of our own day which have had an underlying seriousness.

From then on there have been hundreds of productions in this country alone and most actresses of note have tried Rosalind. One of those who surprisingly did not was Ellen Terry—possibly because before she had the chance to do so Irving had switched to presenting only tragedies. It was something she regretted all her life, towards the end of which she said: 'Would I could say "I have been Rosalind"', would that the opportunity to play this part had come my way when I was in my prime. I reckon it one of the greatest disappointments of my life that it did not. In my old age I go on studying Rosalind rather wistfully, I admit. A contemporary of Shakespeare's writes that "those who are illustrious by long descent reveal their nobility beyond possibility of a mistake. They have in them a simplicity, a naive goodwill, a delicate good feeling that separates them from arrogant assumptions or false noblesse." Of such is Rosalind. It is a beautiful idyll that begins in jest and ends in tender earnest.'

More recent Rosalinds have included Dame Edith Evans, Dame

Peggy Ashcroft, Dorothy Tutin, Eileen Atkins and Vanessa Redgrave. Vanessa Redgrave clutched everybody's heartstrings when she took on the role in 1961/62 in Stratford and London. Said Michael Elliott: 'She can take off her boy's cap and shake sunbeams out of her hair.'

Bernard Levin, writing in the *Express*, went wild: 'And above all enchantment—oh, wonderful, wonderful, most wonderful and after that out of all whooping—Vanessa Redgrave's Rosalind. It is virtually faultless, a creature of fire and light, her voice a golden gate on lapis lazuli hinges, her body a slender reed rippling in the breeze of her love ... this is not acting at all but living, being loved. If the word enchantment has any meaning, it is here.'

The Stratford Rosalind before Vanessa Redgrave was Dame Peggy Ashcroft, who had also played the role in London in 1932. She too moved the critics to rapture. Alan Dent, writing in the *News Chronicle*, said of the 1957 production that Dame Peggy was 'truly ravishing ... so intact and light of touch is her gaiety and youthfulness. The immense charm of her new interpretation lies in the fact that for all its extraordinary virtuoso quality and cunning delineation, the effect should seem so thrillingly spontaneous.' Derek Granger of *The Financial Times* said that she showed how wise was Rosalind in the knowledge of the ways of love. A later Rosalind still was Jane Lapotaire, who came to the part after playing Viola and before playing another role with which both parts have something in common, that of Rosaline in *Love's Labour's Lost*. This is how she sees it:

'Rosalind is the most like Rosaline. Like her, she has all the answers and she never discloses any insecurity or doubts about Orlando's love for her. It's a very long part—the biggest female role in Shakespeare apart from Isabella. There is something very interesting and exciting about Rosalind and Viola, the breeches parts. They only have one scene each in which the audience sees them as women before they get into breeches—then they blossom, they are much more colourful, more adventurous—not surprisingly, I suppose, as the parts were written for boys.

'Rosalind is far more of a prose part than Viola. It is Viola who has all the heartrending lines—she can see herself sitting it out at Orlando's court for years and years, losing her looks, loving the man, never escaping from an intolerable situation. Rosalind has no doubts at all about *her* attraction. She's totally different. She's a great realist. Although she dresses as a man, she never really plays a man. She remains extremely feminine—there is a huge element of fun in her.

'She's wilful, almost coy sometimes, she uses her feminine wiles most overtly and clearly. Rosalind faces no conflict, she never has to prove her masculinity like poor Viola. Rosalind is only involved with a handful of people in her male disguise—Corin, Sylvius, Phebe—but there is no pretence. She does not have to live out her life as does Viola, always living in emotional pain because of her feelings for Orsino. There are differences too in the way they react when women fall in love with them—Rosalind just gets very irate with Phebe and tells her off for treating Corin so badly whereas Viola is stunned and just wonders whatever she is going to do about it.

'Both women are fleeing from disaster and both go on a spiritual journey as well as a physical one. They go to strange lands in strange costumes and disguised as different people. They move entirely out of their own environment. But the crucial thing for me is that Rosalind never becomes a boy at all, her psychology is totally feminine, her attitudes are feminine—she is a fully rounded and understanding woman.'

There is a story that before the last war a production of *Twelfth Night* was being given at the open-air Minack Theatre in Cornwall. During the afternoon performance a fog came down during which a foreign fishing vessel ran aground on the beach below the theatre. The men had no idea where they were when they climbed up the cliff path in front of them and emerged into the second scene of the play just as Viola asks her rescuers, 'What country, friends, is this?' to which the captain replies, 'It is Illyria, lady,' and the bemused fishermen wondered where on earth they were.

Twelfth Night has been called Shakespeare's most perfect play. It is a comedy, but a comedy with great overtones of sadness. Unlike *As You Like It*, events take place in a real world of households, stewards, servants and unwanted relations. It was written at the turn of the century, it is said, especially to be performed before Elizabeth on Twelfth Night 1600. Its first recorded performance, however, is in 1602.

The play links the two halves of Shakespeare's working life. It was the last great comedy before the years of tragedies, and in it appears almost every theme he has used in his previous comedies—the boy/girl disguise, the lost twins who are mistaken for each other, the comic retainers and the woman who falls in love with another woman. It foreshadowed the Puritanism so hated by Elizabethans, it provided low comedy, a classic clown, and the feeling of carnival, of twelfth-night holiday. But the real world is never far off. *As You Like It* finished in a happy romantic pastorale, all couples neatly paired off to live happily ever after, with only Jaques standing outside the idyll of Arden. A cold wind blows through the theatre at the end of *Twelfth Night*. 'Hey, ho, the wind and the rain,' sings Feste to the audience. No doubt Orsino and Viola, Sebastian and Olivia, will live happily ever after, but reality has broken in on everybody else.

Poor Andrew Aguecheek realizes he has been gulled all along. Sir Toby and Maria are married in what Anne Barton rightly describes as 'one of the coldest off-stage bargains'. Malvolio, for whom we now have sympathy, rounds on all of them threatening revenge 'on the whole pack of you', and poor Antonio, in love with Sebastian and prepared to give his life for him, is left bereft, lonely and forgotten. As *The Tempest* seems to sum up the total of Shakespeare's whole working canon, so does *Twelfth Night* end an era.

Its closest source is an Italian play *Gl'Ingannati* (*The Deceived*), written in 1531. Barnabe Rich's story of Apolonius and Silla in *Riche's Farewell to Military Profession* contains the elements of shipwreck, twins of different sexes, the girl disguised as a man and her love for the Duke. Shakespeare had used the twins before in *The Comedy of Errors* (albeit twins of the same sex), but Malvolio is his own truly original creation.

Shakespeare has given Viola some of the most beautiful words he ever wrote for anybody. She is, as has already been said, far more accepting and passive than is Rosalind, but it is she who has the more poetic imagination. Commenting on her, Anne Barton says: 'She simply accepts her strange situation, she does not attempt to transform it, as Rosalind and Julia did. Although she knows that "youth's a stuff will not endure", that her beauty is wasting away in boy's disguise, she insists that "Time must untangle this, not I". Even when the plot seems to demand her interference, as it does at the end of Act III, she sits still, placing her faith in the mysterious symmetries of a universe whose "tempests are kind and salt waves fresh in love". This trust is justified.'

Viola represents true feeling among a positive welter of other kinds of emotion, Orsino's love of being in love, Olivia's wallowing in grief, Malvolio's self-love and Aguecheek's insane fantasies that he is loved by Olivia (who has never given either of them a thought). W. H. Auden found the love of both Viola and Antonio too real and genuine for the play entirely, their emotions too strong when surrounded by such affectations.

As with Rosalind, many famous actresses have played Viola. One problem, of course, is to make a Sebastian look believably like her, and although brothers and sisters have played the roles—such as Mrs Henry Siddons and William Murray in 1815—it does not seem to have been actually played by twins. In some productions one actress has doubled both parts, including Kate Terry in 1865 and Jessica Tandy in 1937. But Viola remains highly popular. As the editors of the Arden edition of *Twelfth Night* say, 'it is a character universally attractive to actresses and audiences alike'.

Ellen Terry was described as showing 'graceful impudence' in the role, but this is not how she saw herself. 'It is a lovely rather than a brilliant mind. Viola is less witty than either Rosalind or Beatrice. She seldom says a clever thing. She often says a beautiful thing. She has put into her mouth some of the most exquisite word music Shakespeare ever wrote. Of her it may be said that "her tongue's sweet airs more tunable than lark to shepherd's ears". This is the Viola that Ada Rehan brought on to a stage.'

It is Viola, she says, with the enduring love, who tells Olivia what she would do:

> Make me a willow cabin at your gate,
> And call upon my soul within the house;

> Write loyal canons of contented love,
> And sing them loud even in the dead of night;
> Halloo your name to the reverberate hills,
> And make the babbling gossip of the air
> Cry out 'Olivia!' O, you should not rest
> Between the elements of air and earth,
> But you should pity me.

'Viola', continues Ellen Terry, 'has a golden heart as well as a golden voice. She listens with tender sympathy and patience to Orsino's rhapsodies about Olivia. Imagine Rosalind or Beatrice in Viola's situation! Could either of them have resisted a jest at the unfortunate Orsino's passion? An honourable and unselfish girl this Viola.'

Other famous Violas have included Barbara Jefford, Dame Peggy, Dorothy Tutin and Diana Rigg, all of whom have brought something of themselves to the part. The 1979 Stratford Viola, Cheri Lunghi, had a very young and luminous charm which was most appealing.

To return to Jane Lapotaire, who played the role at Stratford in 1974; she again compared Rosalind to Viola in respect of Rosalind's feminine wiles. 'Viola does not use any of them.

> My father had a daughter lov'd a man
> As it might be perhaps, were I a woman,
> I should your lordship

is the nearest she ever gets to using them, to being inverted in her situation. Viola does not even have the authority of getting back into women's dress at the end and I found that it always left me with egg on my face, standing next to Orsino, having proclaimed my love but without the chance to demonstrate that I'm actually a woman. Rosalind gets a dress and so completes the cycle.

'Viola takes her boyhood very seriously—she has to in order to survive. She really has to go through with it all the way, which is why the duel scene, although it is very funny, is also painful too because we know her secret. The scene has to be played straight.

'Peter Gill, who directed me, felt that the crucial, most poignant part of Viola's dilemma was the rapid passage of time. Orsino rubs it in:

For women are as roses, whose fair flower,
Being once displayed, doth fall that very hour.

To which Viola replies "And so they are: alas, that they are so."
He told me to go away and think about it and I did. I looked at
photographs of myself in other parts when I was younger and I
thought, yes, My God, he's right. Viola is more fully rounded than
the other two women Rosalind and Rosaline, she has that poignant
vulnerability. But with both Rosalind and Viola I felt when I had
finished playing the roles that I had only just reached the tip of the
iceberg. In all the plays, Shakespeare pays you back a thousandfold
for what you put in.'

One of the most moving Violas of recent years was Judi Dench,
who played her in John Barton's production in Stratford and
London in 1969/70. When a Barton production really works it
continues to grow in depth with the passage of time, and this is
what happened with his *Twelfth Night*. The sound of the sea was
never far away from this Illyria, and the action took place within a
huge Tudor hall lit with multitudes of candles. The whole had a
wonderful autumnal glow.

Charles Thomas, who died tragically during the run of the play,
was her first Orsino, the part later being taken over by Richard
Pasco. 'Charlie was most beautiful, so right for Viola. He
was so memorable, so deeply lyrical. It was his wonderful idea to
come on in the last scene looking like that little Hilliard
miniature with flowers in his hair and the lovelock hanging
down—so beautiful.

'Of course, Viola is one of Shakespeare's most beautiful
roles—there are such depths in it. She is never just a jaunty boy,
she is desperately vulnerable and there are tremendous areas of
great sadness in her although she is the catalyst in the play. Like *all*
Shakespeare's heroines, certainly those in his comedies, she has
grown up by the end of the play; she has grown tremendously in
maturity.

'There, in Viola, you have love. Of the others, Orsino is in love
with love, Olivia is in love with being in mourning, Malvolio is
sick of self-love, Aguecheek thinks he's in love, Maria loves Sir
Toby in a desperate kind of last chance way, and he has a kind of

love for her. Antonio really does love Sebastian—it's a play about every different facet of love.

'I read recently an interview with an actress which really amazed me. She said she felt the kind of love Viola felt for Orsino was something we simply don't understand these days. I found that extraordinary. Perhaps she was misreported but I just couldn't understand it. Because it seems to me in that play, that if you have ever felt love of any kind at all you can look for it there and find an exact parallel. It's contained within the very heart and structure of the play—it is not just a play about love but about how people deal with it, how resilient people are, how selfish, how giving. There you have it—all the facets.'

'They never meet but there is a skirmish of wit between them'

Throughout the line of early comedies there is a type of girl or woman with a very noticeable family resemblance, and who is seen at her most rounded as Beatrice. Beginning with Adriana in *The Comedy of Errors*, through Kate the Shrew and Rosaline of *Love's Labour's Lost* to Beatrice, she moves from scold to lady of spirit, but the seeds of one are there in the others.

Scholars seem to disagree totally over which was written first, *The Comedy of Errors* or *The Taming of the Shrew*. Both were in performance by 1594, so it is likely that they were written during the period 1592/93. *Comedy of Errors* is taken from two plays by Plautus, and its first recorded performance (on 28 December 1594 at Gray's Inn), was followed by a court case. This resulted from 'the great disorders and abuses done and committed during the evening by a company of base or common fellows under the leadership of a sorceror or conjuror'. The sorcerer successfully defended himself and the players by accusing the attorney and solicitor of 'knavery and juggling' in presenting the case.

In the play are themes to which Shakespeare was to return on a number of occasions: twins mistaken for one another (in this case two sets), a shipwreck which separated wife from husband and children from both almost at birth, a coming together at the end of the complete family after all had seemed lost.

Adriana, who has married one of the Antipholus twins, is a scold and is certainly jealous, although when we see the terms her husband is obviously on with the local courtesans it appears she may have cause. Her opening words have a contemporary ring when she discusses with her sister why her husband is so late home for dinner that it is spoilt. Her sister more or less says men will be men, to which Adriana replies 'Why should their liberty than ours be more?', followed by a crisp exchange:

Luciana	Because their business still lies out o' door.
Adriana	Look, when I serve him so he takes it ill.
Luciana	O, know he is the bridle of your will.
Adriana	Then none but asses will be bridled so. . . .

In 1976 Trevor Nunn directed a stunning musical version for the RSC in which Judi Dench played a highly sympathetic Adriana. She not only picked on the wrong twin (her husband's unknown brother) to drag him home to dinner but we were also led to assume she had later lugged him into bed—which made her scandalized query at the end 'Which of you two did dine with me today?' bring down the house.

The source for *The Taming of the Shrew* goes back to classical literature, but the sub-plot of Bianca and her suitors came from a play by Ariosto called *I Suppositi*. There appears to have been an earlier play, *The Taming of A Shrew*, too, which was already popular in 1594, when it was described by the printer, Peter Short, as having been 'at sundry times acted by the Right Honourable the Earle of Pembroke and his servants', according to Dover Wilson. *The Shrew* was a play which suffered a good deal at the hands of seventeenth- and eighteenth-century adaptors, and even Garrick produced his own version, *Catherine and Petruchio*. In this the leading parts were played by Kitty Clive and Henry Woodward, who were notorious for their off-stage quarrels, which gave the play an added edge. There are reports that he threw her on the floor so hard that he knocked the breath out of her, that she went for him on another occasion with her nails and that once he stuck a fork in her finger.

To some women today *The Shrew* appears to be an unpleasant play all about the subjugation of women, but this seems to depend on how you read the text. In 1979 Michael Bogdanov directed a production which was set in a Mafia-type 1930s Italy, where all the relationships were translated into cash terms and where Kate was totally beaten into abject submission at the end. The result was not only distasteful but seemed contrary to the spirit of the play. (It did show up Kate's sister Bianca, however, as the little cat she is.)

Dame Peggy Ashcroft put her finger on the nub of *The Shrew* when she said that the overriding fact is that Kate actually falls in love with Petruchio at first sight, and everything she does stems from that.

Alan Cookson, writing in *The Tatler*, said of Peggy Ashcroft's performance as Kate: 'Her view of Kate is that of a headstrong girl with a loving heart. She is a girl of spirit and she is waiting for a man of spirit and an even stronger will than her own to get the better of her. Beneath her indulged wilfulness and violence of temper there is a wish to be subdued and she is willing to suffer stoically in the process of subjugation.

'She does not spare the shrewishness . . . but the beauty of her playing is that she is alive, sometimes almost pathetically so, to every move of the game. She has been in love with Petruchio all along and recognises clearly that he is only playing the bully. She waits patiently for him to play out his part and when the time comes sees to it that the reconciliation is a true reconciliation of temperament. There is no suggestion that Kate in her sermon is slyly laughing at the man who supposes he has mistreated her.'

Certainly actresses who have played the part do not feel they have been really tamed at the end of the play.

Jane Lapotaire feels 'it is perverse to change the meaning of the play. Katharina is an intelligent woman. All her father has done is to present her with a selection of idiots from which to choose a husband. She's wilful and a real woman and there is no problem in portraying her.

'I feel she falls in love almost immediately with Petruchio but she must fight him on her own level. He's met his mistress, too, and half-way through the play they begin to grasp how serious they really are about each other. It is essential to put over a huge sense of fun. We hoped that the audience would realize the true situation from the word go and then go along with it. You must not send up the part. You have to give all your life and energy to the battles in which you join, remembering that both have met their match and therefore fight as equals.

'Even though it is called *The Taming of the Shrew*, I very much doubt that even in Shakespeare's day it was taken at its face value, shrew meets match and is broken by him. They must have laughed more at a boy playing the part of a scolding woman, but even taking into account the Elizabethan attitude, Kate is not a stereotyped female shrew.

'If you turn it into a sadistic exercise as the last production did at the RSC then it becomes totally unacceptable and makes absolute nonsense of the last speech and "Kiss me Kate." Shakespeare actually ensures at the end that Kate maintains a woman's dignity, she's a complete character. He is the first man she has met who is witty, intelligent; he is a valid partner for her and you can see they will have a continuing relationship when the play ends. If Snakespeare had wanted her to be broken and destroyed he would have written it that way. The speech at the end is deliberately fulsome, she won't let him down in public and they both know what she's playing at.'

To Janet Suzman, Kate is very young. 'Kate's got no excuse for behaving so atrociously unless she's an adolescent—a fully grown woman could not possibly get away with that kind of behaviour.

'In that scene about the moon and the sun we made a useful discovery; if you can laugh *with* somebody you can't fight them any more. What Petruchio is doing in that scene is teaching Kate a small lesson in humour. We found a particular moment when she realizes what he's up to; the penny drops, and she changes. This farouche, temperamental, self-defensive girl, unsmiling and quick-brained, suddenly sees the joke, throws back her head, lets go, and laughs and laughs and laughs. Petruchio, over the moon (so to speak!) that his exhausting game has been seen through at long last, joins her. Their love—combative, spirited, and until this moment, unspoken—can now flourish. Each has found an ally. Her pride has been restored. That hyperbolic speech at the end of the play, reviled by feminists, can now become Kate playing, in public, the exact game she has been taught in private. It is a paean to the secretiveness of real passion. And remember—Petruchio *always* stops before anything dangerous happens; no harm ever comes to Kate, does it?'

Love's Labour's Lost appeared in Quarto in 1598, but was known to have been performed for some time before that. It is generally dated 1593/95, making it approximately contemporary with the Sonnets; the Dark Lady of the Sonnets and Rosaline in *Love's Labour's Lost* are considered by some to be one and the same.

There is no known source for the play, and there have been many arguments as to its contemporary allusions and in-jokes. The names of some of the characters are those of real people, although Shakespeare's portrayals were not in the least like the real thing.

The plot is very simple. The King of Navarre and three young men take to the forest and swear to give up women and devote themselves to learning for three years. Their plan goes awry when the Princess of France and three young ladies (one of whom is Rosaline) also choose to make a temporary home in the forest. The comedy lies in the gradual weakening of one man after the other, which comes to a climax in the marvellous scene where the hypocritical Berowne—who has berated all the others for falling by the wayside—is caught in his own net. A love-letter he has written to Rosaline has become confused with a document on its way to the King, and when it arrives it is handed to him by the King to be read out loud. The play ends on an unexpectedly sombre note with the arrival of a messenger to tell the Princess that her father is dead and she is Queen, and the men are sent away on various onerous tasks until a long period of mourning is done.

Rosaline is neither a scold nor a shrew, but she seems to be a very unsentimental and tough-minded lady—she never appears to soften towards Berowne, nor do we see much sign of her vulnerability. When she sends him off at the end of the play—to make sick people laugh with his humour—the text does not make it clear whether she cares or not. Actresses differ as to their own feelings about this. Some seem to prefer to leave the question of her feelings open; others, like Janet Suzman, feel that she does care, and that you should get that across.

Rosaline is one of the few Shakespeare heroines whose colouring we know. Berowne says of her that she is 'whitely wanton, with a velvet brow, with two pitch-balls stuck in her face for eyes', which certainly has overtones of the Dark Lady. To be called 'dark' or 'black' was something of an insult at this point in time, when the epitome of feminine beauty was—as has often been the case since—the blue-eyed, pink-cheeked blonde.

She is a woman about whom actresses seem to have reservations, although Janet Suzman describes her as 'a cracker, one of the best. She and Berowne are the most complete couple in the play, and are on the way to becoming Beatrice and Benedick. I find, in both characters, their moral character to be very attractive.'

Jane Lapotaire says that Rosaline 'is a kind of hors d'œuvre before the great roles like Rosalind and Beatrice. Rosaline is totally self-possessed and upbeat. She always wins hands down. There is no character comparison—there is none of the vulnerability of Viola or the poignance of a Rosalind.

'I think she's uncomfortable for women these days. She's the only Shakespearean woman who does not have to earn her place. He gives those four women all the cards and all they have to do is play them.

'Has she altered by the end of the play?—well, perhaps. When she says to Berowne well, if you think you're so funny go and make sick people laugh perhaps there is an insecurity. Is he really serious about her? Perhaps somewhere there is a feeling in her that she is not so sure of him in spite of the sexuality she wears like armour.'

George Bernard Shaw had a low opinion of *Much Ado About Nothing*, but then he tended to have low opinions of any comedy not written by G. B. Shaw. 'The main pretension in *Much Ado*', he says, 'is that Benedick and Beatrice are exquisitely witty and amusing persons. They are, of course, nothing of the sort. Benedick's pleasantries might pass at a sing-song in a public house parlour.'

As to Beatrice, 'in her character of a professed wit she has only one subject, and that is the subject which a really witty woman never jests about, because it is too serious a matter to a woman to be made light of without indelicacy. Beatrice jests about it for the sake of the indelicacy. There is only one thing worse than the Elizabethan "merry gentleman" and that is the Elizabethan "merry lady".'

The play appears to have been written in 1598/99. The Claudio/Hero plot was similarly a story Shakespeare would use again, in *Othello*, *The Winter's Tale* and *Cymbeline*—the woman slandered by mischief-makers whose lover or husband is led to believe she has been unfaithful to him. Beatrice and Benedick seem to be Shakespeare's own creations, and there have been plenty of examples of couples who have fallen in love with each other once the idea has been put into their minds.

Of Ellen Terry's performance Bernard Shaw said, 'Your Beatrice is a rather creditable performance, considering that I didn't stage manage it.' Ellen Terry said herself, '"By my troth a pleasant-spirited lady" says Don Pedro. The actress who impersonates Beatrice should remember that testimonial. Beatrice's repartee in her encounters with Benedick can easily be made to sound malicious and vulgar. It should be spoken with the lightest raillery, with mirth in the voice and charm in the manner.

'Here are two people strongly attracted by one another and unwilling to admit it because both are afraid of the admission being laughed at.'

For her, the highspot of the play comes when Beatrice defends her friend Hero then calls on Benedick to kill his friend for slandering her. 'Beatrice comes forward and unpacks her heart. They are very difficult words for an actress. I have played Beatrice hundreds of times and never done this speech as I feel it should be done.

'This wonderful scene throws such a flood of light on Beatrice's character that an actress has little excuse for not seeing clearly what kind of woman she had to impersonate.' She goes on to say sadly that when she took on the role she inherited a lot of stage business she did not think at all funny or in keeping with the character, but was told by Irving that she had to play it that way because that was the way it had always been played. Finally she says 'I have played Beatrice hundreds of times, but not once as I know she ought to be played. I was not swift enough . . . but at least I did not make the mistake of being arch and skittish.'

Dame Peggy Ashcroft was one of the great Beatrices—she played it opposite Sir John Gielgud first in 1950. 'Again I think of Beatrice as a girl. I think Judi [Dench] played the most brilliant Beatrice—she played her as someone on the verge of spinsterhood. I made her younger.

'Beatrice is what I would call a natural. She speaks before she thinks. I know that what I felt about her when I was playing her was that instead of being a witty woman who can always say the smart thing, she just happens to say what comes into her head and it's spot on. She is merry, unpredictable, undisciplined, the poor relation who isn't a poor relation—she doesn't give a damn whether she gets a husband or not, and she's a mocker.

'Then she's caught in her own trap, and she's full of heart. She's a lovely character—but then the great thing about Shakespeare, the theatre and acting is that there is no one way to play a part, you have your own approach to playing roles and thank God because we can go on seeing the plays for ever and every Beatrice and every Benedick is a different interpretation.'

Janet Suzman says: 'Beatrice I did really love. I love her defiance. She's *damned* if she's going to admit she loves the man. She's got something so crystalline, so witty, so tough, yet underneath she's soft and vulnerable. She is one of the many women in Shakespeare who shows incredible loyalty and friendship for another woman. It is Beatrice, in that astonishing scene, who asks Benedick to kill Claudio; asks him, in effect, to change sides.

'Yes, I think Beatrice and Benedick had some kind of relationship before the play begins. Shakespeare's comedic touch is infallible—there's her friend getting married, much younger than her, and suddenly Beatrice doesn't feel well ... she gets a cold. Beatrice is a grown woman, at *least* in her twenties—unlike pubertal Kate.'

Judi Dench played Beatrice in 1976 in a production by John Barton which he set in Victorian India, and which she found very difficult to come to terms with at first.

'I found it hard because a lot of the language is really very racy, especially in the morning scene between the two girls. They speak to each other most frankly, and I thought that they would never have spoken like that in corsets, in a period when they were still covering up the legs of pianos. I found that so difficult, but I overcame it because John did create a terribly real household.

'In a way, Beatrice is very Shavian, she's a Shaw's girl and not quite like the other Shakespeare girls at all. She actually speaks more like one of the chaps. The clue to how I played her was the one line when she says of Benedick that he played me false before. I think there was a big, big thing between them—it almost says it—and something went desperately wrong. Had it not been for that one summer they would have remained a bachelor and a spinster all their lives.

'I'd never read the play before, although I'd seen Liz Spriggs play it and thought she was marvellous. Beatrice is funny, witty, so vulnerable watching her friend's wedding preparations, getting a psychosomatic cold. She's a deeply hurt, sad girl. The dance at the end of the play is a wonderful celebration of the end of her spinsterhood.'

As Anne Barton says, 'Beatrice and Benedick remain within the flawed society which has fostered them and brought them together. Their relationship, however, is one they have created for themselves and it suggests an alternative mode of love to that of the "model" couple Hero and Claudio: ragged, humorous, a bit undignified, demanding, but also individual and emotionally realised as the other is not.'

Perhaps Dover Wilson summed up Beatrice best. 'Beatrice is the first woman in our literature, perhaps in the literature of Europe, who not only has a brain, but delights in the constant employment of it.'

'How would you be if he, which is the top of judgement, should but judge you as you are?'

In Portia and Isabella we see most clearly the changing fashions in the popularity of Shakespeare's heroines. Isabella was highly approved of in Victorian times—not surprisingly—became a character very distasteful to modern ways of thought and then recently has begun to intrigue actresses as to her personality and motivation. Portia, on the other hand, was previously always one of Shakespeare's most popular female roles, yet, as Dame Peggy Ashcroft confirms, she seems to have lost popularity with many young actresses today.

Portia, however, has her devotees, as we shall see. *The Merchant of Venice* may have been written in 1596, following a highly successful revival of Marlowe's *The Jew of Malta*. Anti-semitism was in the air, for it was in 1594 that Dr Lopez, a Portuguese Jew and personal doctor to Queen Elizabeth, was brought to trial and executed for plotting to poison the Queen on orders from Spain. Although he was convicted, there seems doubt as to whether he was guilty—not the least of those showing doubt at the time was the Queen herself. However, it made the character of a horrid Jew a popular one.

Possibly one of the reasons for the diminishing popularity of Portia today is the overriding guilt we feel about the treatment of Jews, although Shakespeare does actually go some way towards expressing Shylock's point of view when he makes the latter say: 'I am a Jew. Hath not a Jew eyes? hath not a Jew hands, organs, dimensions, senses, affections, passions? . . . If you prick us do we not bleed?'

Apart from the topical story, Shakespeare's other sources appear to have been an Italian tale in a collection called *Il Pecerone* and another in *Gesta Romanorum* when a trial for love is in fact reversed and it is the girl who has to choose between a gold, silver or lead vessel—a common folk tale.

Ellen Terry loved Portia, playing the role almost to the end of her acting career. To her the sources for the story were irrelevant. 'What does matter is that the genius of the man enabled him in *The Merchant of Venice* to give the very echo to the place where the Adriatic is enthroned. That is why I believe in representing Portia as a Venetian lady. There are many different ways of playing the part. I have tried five or six ways but I have always come back to the Italian way, the Renaissance way.' She goes on to point out that traditionally Portia was played in Germany up to her own time as a low comedy part, complete with moustache.

'Portia is the fruit of the Renaissance, the child of a period of beautiful clothes, beautiful cities, beautiful ideas. She speaks the beautiful language of inspired poetry. Wreck that beauty and the part goes to pieces.

'George Brandes, the Shakespearean commentator, summed up Portia's character as well as it can be done when he writes that "in spite of her self surrender in love there is something independent, almost masculine, in her attitude to life". The orphan heiress has been in a position of authority since childhood. She is used to acting on her own responsibility without seeking advice first. It makes me rather impatient when I am told that it is strange that a woman of this type, in the habit of directing herself and directing others, should be willing to be directed by a man so manifestly inferior to her as Bassanio. I think if we take the trouble to enquire into the motives at the back of the famous speech of surrender it will not strike us as either strange or repellent.

'Remember that Portia so far has had everything given to her. She is the spoiled child of fortune, or would be if she were not so generous. It is this excessive generosity which partly explains her offering with herself all she has to the man she loves. *Noblesse oblige* was not an empty phrase in her day.' However, Ellen Terry goes on to point out that even so Portia retains her independence of thought and action to the point of making plans to save Antonio's life without so much 'as a with your leave or by your leave to her lord and master!'

'I have often been asked whether I think Portia's line of pleading in the court is her own. Was the quibble by which she destroys Shylock's case, and so saves Antonio, her own idea or did it originate from the learned Bellario? The question interests me more than the one as to whether the quibble was justified. . . . Desperate evils demand desperate remedies.'

So who thought of the trap? 'It is my belief that it was not a man. I have an idea that the learned Bellario told Portia at once that the law could not help Antonio, and told her to appeal to Shylock's mercy, and if that failed, his cupidity. If *that* failed, try a threat. To my mind, and I have always tried to show this in the trial scene, Portia is acting on a preconcerted plan up to the moment of pronouncing sentence, then she has the inspiration and acts on it. Hence her "tarry a little". There has flashed through her brain suddenly the thought that a pound of flesh is not the same thing as a pound of flesh and blood. She has to try and disguise her apprehension that this may be a distinction without a difference. . . . I am convinced that this bit of casuistry was not conceived by Shakespeare as being carefully planned. It strikes me as a lightning-like inspiration—just such an inspiration as a woman might have when she is at her wit's end and is willing to try anything to avoid defeat.' Even in Ellen Terry's day, sympathy had begun to swing towards Shylock, but 'to me, Portia will always be a thing "enskied and sainted". I often pray that to the end of my life I may be able to do some justice to these inspired words.'

Barbara Jefford is an actress who has also enjoyed playing Portia. 'I enjoyed her each time I played it—the first time I was about twenty-seven, then thirty-four and then forty-three and not only did I enjoy it each time, I found it easier to bridge the gaps in the character. Portia's in two plays, and never the twain really meet. They do not seem to add up, so you have to make them add up. She is a very clever girl and a frivolous lady as well. She's very unexpected. On her previous showing, her track record would not lead you to believe that she could suddenly turn on the performance she gives in the court scene.

'When you listen to what people say about her, they don't say she's immensely clever or renowned for her wit and intellect, they say, she's very beautiful, fair and richly left, all the pleasant things you can say about an heiress. She is never given a great build-up for her wit, like Beatrice (and that's a hard thing to match up to when you come on, I might say . . .). It is the dual aspect of Portia which makes it so interesting to play. As in all Shakespeare's women roles, there is so much leeway, the thing is to find your own ways around them.

'Standing up to Shylock in the trial scene is a most formidable task. It is extraordinary when you think that Henry Irving used to finish the play after the trial scene! I suppose he felt the rest of the play was nothing because he wasn't in it and he was the Actor Manager. The rest was just the love interest and so on; all that lovely poetry and the marvellous funny scene at the end went for nothing. It just finished with him stamping off—with a great howl.

'I had not realized that Ellen Terry saw it the same way, but I agree about the pound of flesh. It suddenly comes to her, and must be done as a stunning brainwave, the luckiest thing. It's really touch and go—that's the way it seems to work as you're playing it. Yes, she would have been briefed. She has absolutely all the facts and knows exactly how to present them. The formidable old chap won't give an inch, and she probably didn't expect it would be like that, he was just a seedy old money-lender, then she finds he is absolutely manic, possessed by the desire for revenge.

'I don't find Bassanio a suitable husband for her at all. His wooing is so contrived, and it is very difficult to make it believable. In Michael Benthall's production, the first time I did it, he managed the casket scenes very well. He was rather free with Shakespeare—not for nothing was he known as Slasher Benthall. But he juxtaposed the wooing scenes and had them, one, two, three, with no scenes in between, which made it better somehow, more believable. If you start thinking about it then you don't believe it. But really Bassanio is quite awful—if you think some of the heroines, like Hero, are wet then what about the men? He is little more than an outright fortune-hunter and really doesn't hold up as a hero any more than that dreadful Bertram in *All's Well*.'

Dame Peggy Ashcroft is also very fond of Portia, 'even if she no longer seems to be very popular with actresses, especially the younger generation, just now'. She does not see the two sides of the character as being so far apart: 'It is the actress's job to make a character whole. Portia belongs to the adventurous heroines of Shakespeare. She is much more adventurous than, say, Viola, as Viola assumes her character as a boy because there is nothing else she can really do, it was the only way she could carry on having reached Illyria.

'The first time I played Portia I felt I had to really get down and find out what lay behind that first line "By my troth, Nerissa, my little body is aweary of this great world." You see, it can be played by a languid lady—I'd seen it done, played by middle-aged languid ladies all sighs and my little body is aweary and so on, but this is not how I saw it. There's a sort of *impatience* about Portia, she is fed up at being caged by her father's will, she is put into this mould which she resents and I am quite sure that she fixes it so that Arragon and Morocco are not going to get her. Maybe there's a little nervousness but I think she would always have got out of it.

'Then she is in love with Bassanio, and she's appalled at the situation his friend is in. I think one has to take the *Merchant of Venice* as a wonderful fairy tale, but a fairy tale for real. She has to completely assume the personality of that young lawyer. She's been to Bellario and she has got the whole thing taped by the time she comes into court. She knows there is a loophole over the blood, and if it is not mentioned in the Bond then she knows it will be all right.

'Of course she's nervous—are they going to recognize her? Will they see through her? But she's a very clever girl, and she starts out at the beginning of the trial scene to make her immediate plea, the Jew must be merciful. She presumes he will do the right thing—he doesn't. She puts it to him several times. Then she says—and this I think is a moment of nervousness—"prithee let me look upon the Bond". And he gives it to her and she knows it's all right. Then she plays him again—'Shylock, here's thrice thy money'. She gives him three chances to be merciful and then she strikes. She plays that devilish trick on him. There are those who say that Portia is extremely cruel both to Shylock and Antonio but I do not agree because she brings him to the point of admitting that he wants to

murder Antonio, she proves her case. She can only do it in that
way, by saying

> A pound of that same merchant's flesh is thine;
> The court awards it, and the law doth give it

and

> And you must cut this flesh from off his breast;
> The law allows it, and the court awards it.

He becomes more and more excited ('a sentence, come prepare')
then, of course, comes 'Tarry a little, there is something else.'

'Then she's won. She's proved that he's a murderer, she's done
the trick. I think the trial scene is a very thrilling scene indeed.
People tend to say nowadays that it is ridiculous and so on but
people do suspend their disbelief if you really believe it yourself.
Portia is enormously fascinating, exciting and fun.'

All that Isabella and Portia have in common is that it falls on both
of them to find themselves pleading to save a life. From the
fairy-tale atmosphere of Belmont it is a long way to the dark
byways of Isabella's Vienna. *Measure for Measure* is variously
described as a problem play and a black comedy. The likely date
for the play is 1603/4, immediately after *All's Well*, and for his
source Shakespeare went to Cinthio's *Hecatommithi*, and possibly to
a later, dramatized version of this, George Whetstone's *Promos and
Cassandra*.

Basically, the plot is that the Duke of Vienna announces he is
going away on a journey, leaving the state in charge of his
puritanical Deputy, Angelo. In fact the Duke remains in Vienna
disguised as a friar. Angelo stamps down on every kind of vice,
closes down gaming houses and brothels and resurrects a law
whereby any man who gets a girl pregnant is put to death. Such
a one is Claudio, who fully intends marriage—the girl is his
fiancée—but it makes no difference. His sister, Isabella, who is
about to become a nun, is persuaded to go to plead for her brother's
life. She does so, and the cold Angelo is overcome with desire for
her. He suggests that he will give her her brother's life in exchange
for her chastity.

Appalled, she tells her brother, assuming he will readily give up his life for his sister's honour, but not surprisingly he sees it differently. Meanwhile she is taking advice from the disguised Duke, and the bed switch, as in *All's Well*, is worked on Angelo, the lady in question having once been affianced to him. Angelo does not even keep his part of the bargain; he still orders Claudio's execution. However, the Duke arranges another substitution and the head of a prisoner who has died in gaol is presented to Angelo instead of that of Claudio.

It is then announced that the Duke is coming home, and Isabella immediately comes to see him to tell him what has happened. Angelo denies it, saying she is mad, whereupon the Duke reveals himself. Angelo's own life now hangs on Isabella's pleading— which she does, if reluctantly. He marries Mariana, the lady of the bed switch, Claudio is found to be alive after all and, most surprisingly, the Duke asks Isabella to marry him and she presumably agrees.

For a long time Isabella was held up as a fine example of chastity. Not surprisingly she was a firm favourite with Mrs Jameson, who manages an entire chapter on her without ever explaining the nature of the bargain Angelo tries to make with her. But during this century Isabella has not had a good press. Quiller-Couch says she is 'a study in the ugliness of Puritan hypocrisy'.

Robert Speaight feels that it is right that Isabella says nothing to the Duke's proposal. 'Dr Jonathan Miller had her abruptly return to her convent—which is, of course, exactly what she would have done in real life, if real life had brought her into that improbable situation . . . The modern audience, which is rightly reluctant to let Isabella marry the Duke, wrongly forbids her to place a higher price on her own virginity than on her brother's life. "More than our brother is our chastity" is the stiffest hurdle that any actress feels called upon to face; you see them approaching it like a nervous steeplechaser.'

J. W. Lever in the introduction to the Arden edition is more charitable, feeling that Isabella falls into the category described by a writer of Shakespeare's own time who labelled some girls who wanted to be nuns as those who would 'professe and vowe perpetuall chastyte before they suffyciently knowe themselves and the infirmitie of theyre nature'. J. W. Lever continues: 'Youth, ignorance, her confusion of principle and impulse make Isabel's very virtue dangerous to others equally blind to the working of their inner selves and shape her as a perfect example of Angelo's undoing.'

Isabella's desire for a stricter restraint in an ancient and austere order of nuns suggests immature enthusiasm, although 'Isabella's vocation as a nun had seemed doubtful from the very first scene where she appears, perhaps from the first line she spoke.' When she tells her brother of the bargain and expects his sympathy he reacts in the most human way with "Ay, but to die, and go we know not where!" 'To this extremity Isabella's passion for spiritual absolutes, her craving to be a thing "enskied and sainted", have led her. A real-life Isabella, even in Shakespeare's day, would have received scant sympathy from Shakespeare's contemporaries, but she was accepted within the context of the drama. It is in the nature of the play that Isabella's personality, like those of Claudio and Angelo, should seem neither good nor bad but basically self ignorant.' Lever sees Isabella's marriage to the Duke as her true destiny.

Barry Kyle in his 1979 production of the play for the Royal Shakespeare Company had Isabella obviously rushing in to being a nun without stopping to think about it, and he showed her and the Duke becoming drawn to each other through the plots and subterfuges in which they become involved, so that his proposal at the end seemed the natural thing to happen.

Two actresses who see the role differently are Barbara Jefford and Jane Lapotaire. Barbara Jefford 'first played it at nineteen, then again when I was twenty-seven. I don't think I was as good the second time. I think it is probably one of those parts which it is better not to think about too much, you must just take her for granted.

'I don't think you can reason Isabella. Once you start pondering over it and have doubts about virginity and purity and incorruptibility, any doubts at all in fact, then you cannot possibly refuse to save your brother's life. Any kind of sophistication is wrong for Isabella. She must believe in what she does absolutely, even if it means her brother's death—there are no twists in her. I have seen it played as a kind of bluestocking lady who has thought it all out and weighed it up but I don't believe you can do that. You must believe that she has absolutely no choice, and that there is only one way in which she can behave.

'This gives you the passion that carries the whole thing through, which is why it is easier to play when you are very young—you have such tremendous certainty then. The parallel is rather like what happens when you start in this profession—you are quite certain that the way you are doing it is right or you wouldn't be doing it, technique doesn't come into it, just passion, and I think that's what Isabella's about. It's very difficult to simulate that kind of innocence without making her totally unsympathetic.'

For Jane Lapotaire 'the problem you have to solve is why she wants to be a nun. Whatever psychological explanation you come up with, it's got to be watertight for you. The audience don't need to know what it is, but you have to, and then you work the part up from there. Most women think, "I don't want to play that stuck-up virgin who won't sleep with a man to save her brother's life, it's ridiculous" so you have to decide why she wants to go into the convent since it's never made explicit.

'I thought perhaps something sexual had happened to Isabella in her youth, perhaps something to do with her father, and the very closeness she felt for her brother meant she could not bring herself to tell him, it shocked her so much. There is no social reason for her to go into a convent, none of the reasons women went in for in those days—she was wealthy, an only daughter, in no way do you feel she has any kind of vocation. What reasons she gives don't hold water. Shakespeare was not an orthodox Christian and he gives her no orthodox beliefs.

'I think she's an extremely passionate woman. Shakespeare gives her some of the most wonderfully vivid and passionate speeches he ever wrote for women at all. There is a parallel between her and the Duke, he is also at odds with himself and he's also on some kind of journey of self-discovery and, like Isabella and Angelo, he is finally brought face to face with something he has been trying to avoid.

'Isabella has such poetry, such authority, her words have such amazing imagery—that's what turns Angelo on so much, not that she is beautiful, but her energy and passion channelled into chastising him. It makes him think what it would be like channelled into a fulfilled female. The convent was an escape from something she did not want to confront, and Shakespeare rubs her nose right into it. The Order of the Poor Clares was an extremely tough Order, and that she asks if it can be tougher is a real giveaway, in fact it is a very arrogant attitude for a truly vocated girl. It shows her passionate attitude to everything. I do not think she should be too young either, she only packs the weight if she can be seen as a woman who is mature.

'To me it is right that at the end she accepts the Duke. She has made a similar journey into self-discovery. They are oddly suited and she is the right woman for him. In fact I'd go further and say they are ideally suited.'

'For several virtues have I lik'd several women'

As well as the young women around whom so much of the action concentrates in so many of the plays—such as Rosalind, Viola, Beatrice, Isabella—Shakespeare also wrote charming parts for a number of other girls. These could be characters in their own right, like Olivia in *Twelfth Night*, Helena and Hermia in *A Midsummer Night's Dream*; friends, confidantes and foils to other women such as Celia in *As You Like It*, Nerissa in *The Merchant of Venice*; or a combination of foil and the need to further the plot—Hero in *Much Ado About Nothing*. Opinions are divided about Jessica as to just how charming she might be, but she is necessary to the sub-plot of *The Merchant*.

Helena and Hermia both have family resemblances to other Shakespearean girls. Helena not only has the same name as the heroine of *All's Well That Ends Well*; she also shares a desire to pursue her man relentlessly, whether he wants her or not. Hermia, in her defiance of her father and her determination to marry the man of her choice, is a slighter version of Juliet or Desdemona. But both the girls in the *Dream* are people in their own right.

So far as can be ascertained, there is no known source for *A Midsummer Night's Dream*, although of course fairy-tales were still popular in Shakespeare's day, and Puck, Lob, Robin Goodfellow or whatever regional name he went under, would have been a well-known character. Much later than Shakespeare, bowls of cream or little cakes were still left out for Puck, even as they were for the Cornish piskies right into the nineteenth century. The play is thought to have been written in 1595, as Titania's long speech about the devastation of the countryside through dreadful weather is assumed to refer to the bad winter of 1594. That it was specifically written for a wedding also seems likely, and one such event put forward is that of William Stanley, Earl of Derby, to Lady Elizabeth Vere, Burghley's grand-daughter and Queen Elizabeth's own godchild. The whole play is about marriage— Theseus to Hippolyta, Helena to Demetrius, Hermia to Lysander and, of course, the fractured relationship of Oberon and Titania which causes all the confusions of the plot.

We learn at the outset that Helena and Hermia have been friends since babyhood. Helena was wooed by Demetrius, on whom she dotes, but he has since transferred his affection to her friend. Hermia's father likes the match and seeks to force his daughter into it. She is just as determined to wed Lysander, and at the outset of the play makes plans with him to elope. Such is Lysander's faith in Helena's friendship to Hermia that he tells her of the plan, and she (for reasons none too sure) decides to tell Demetrius, although one imagines her turn would have been better served by Hermia's removal from the scene and marriage. Still, it was obviously necessary to get all four into the wood near Athens. Here they will become unwittingly involved in the war between Titania and Oberon and the mischief and mistakes of Puck.

Just as *Two Gentlemen of Verona* had something to say about the friendships of adolescent boys or young men when infatuation intervenes, the quarrel scene in the *Dream* does something similar for girls. The fact that it comes about directly as the result of the mistake made by Puck in putting the love juice on to Lysander's eyes, instead of those of Demetrius, does not detract from the point that once the girls actually turn on each other and let rip, friendship is forgotten and they proceed to dredge up all kinds of insults, from those dealing with physical appearance to nasty reminiscences of nursery days. Indeed, as Proteus said in *The Two Gentlemen of Verona*, in love who respects friend?

Harold Brooks in his introduction to the Arden edition of the play draws attention to the physical appearance of these two girls (already mentioned in Chapter 1), obviously written with two specific lads in mind, one tall and fair, the other small and dark. He says 'They are strongly contrasted in temperament. Hermia is warm-blooded and spirited, tender in happy love, hot and militant in anger; Helena is much more of a lady, very feminine and very much aware of it. Though she cannot forbear to pursue Demetrius, the pursuit offends her womanhood.'

Helena is, in fact, suffering from a common human condition. She has lost self-respect because she has been jilted, and jilted after the kind of promises the exchange of which virtually constituted a betrothal in Elizabethan times. She does not blame her friend for this in the early part of the play. That Demetrius had pursued Helena was well known. Lysander says:

> Demetrius, I'll avouch it to his head,
> Made love to Nedar's daughter, Helena,
> And won her soul: and she (sweet Lady) dotes,
> Devoutly dotes, dotes in idolatry,
> Upon this spotted and inconstant man.

and when Demetrius says that he now loves Hermia instead, Lysander retorts

> You have her father's love, Demetrius:
> Let me have Hermia's: do you marry him.

By the time the mix-up has occurred, and both Demetrius and the bewitched Lysander are now pursuing Helena, the girls' friendship has dissolved with it. Memories of two little girls sitting side by side making a sampler creating 'both one flower' and 'sitting on one cushion, both warbling of one song'—yet these girls who 'grew together like a double cherry', they of 'two seeming bodies, but one heart', can't wait to get at each other.

To return to Brooks's comments. The girls display during the quarrel scene 'traits which are not new developments but which the events of the play have not led them to display before. Aggression with Helena takes the form of cattiness. She knows where Hermia is vulnerable.' Hermia is very conscious of what she considers to be her bad points, and already the bewitched Lysander has attacked her unfashionable dark complexion. Taking her cue from him, Helena attacks the other weak spot, her lack of inches. This brings about Hermia's famous riposte, when she screams at Helena that she looks like a painted maypole.

Helena knows Hermia very well, and, as Brooks says, she is fully aware 'that Hermia's hot temper can be reckoned on for an outburst which will enable her to be characterized as "curs't and shrewish"; a type of female personality particularly obnoxious to men. The master stroke is "she was a vixen when she went to school", making the men visualize instead of the grown-up lady ripe for admiration and love, an undignified demon of a small child under tutelage. Hermia's fury means Helena can capitalize on her feminine need for protection.'

Poor Hermia—she alone realizes that something is sadly out of joint. Says Helena

> Your hands than mine, are quicker for a fray,
> My legs are longer though to run away.

It is Hermia whose words finish this marvellously constructed scene with 'I am amaz'd, and know not what to say.'

Again one wonders how they will fare after the play ends. No doubt Lysander and Hermia will develop their relationship which began with the start of the play and head for a happy marriage. Demetrius and Helena are successfully paired off too, but Helena will always live with the memory of her mad pursuit. As for Demetrius, I have never seen the point made, but it is pertinent that he alone of those bewitched by Oberon's magic flower does not have the love juice removed. As he was not in love with Helena at the beginning—or at least had swung away from her in his affections—he presumably has to remain bewitched while Lysander is made right again and returns to his original love.

There is not a great deal one can say about Hero in *Much Ado About Nothing*. She is one of Shakespeare's suffering, unjustly accused women. Like Hermione and Desdemona, she is wrongly accused of infidelity, and in her case is literally repudiated at the church door. Unlike the other two, her fate is not tragic, and she marries Claudio in the end—although one might ask who would want him after all that?—but her main purpose is to carry along the plot.

Presumably she has enough about her to attract the friendship of the intelligent and lively Beatrice—a gentle foil for her brightness, no doubt—and that there is indeed true friendship

Rosalind: Mrs Abington (1785)

Left. Rosalind: Peggy Ashcroft (1957)

Below. Rosalind: Vanessa Redgrave (1961)

Right. Viola: Ada Rehan (1893)

Far right. Viola: Phillida Terson (1910)

Below right. Viola: Judi Dench (1969)

Left. Rosaline: Jane Lapotaire (1978)

Right. Katharina: Laurence Olivier (1922)

Below: Katharina: Janet Suzman (1967)

Above left. Beatrice: Mrs Mowatt
(?1848)

Above right. Beatrice: Ellen Terry
(1887)

Left. Beatrice: Judi Dench (1976)

Opposite above. Portia: Ellen Terry
(1879)

Opposite below. Portia: Peggy
Ashcroft (1938)

Above left. Isabella: Barbara Jefford (1950)

Above right. Queen Margaret: Peggy Ashcroft (1964)

Left. Hermione: Judi Dench (1969)

between them is shown when Beatrice stands up for her against all accusations. Like Paulina over Hermione and Emilia over Desdemona, Beatrice will not hear what she knows to be an unjust accusation bandied about her friend. In fact, she rages that she is not a man and able to take up weapons on her behalf. But necessary as Hero is to be the second girl in the play it is not a rewarding role to act. 'A dull and boring girl', is how Barbara Jefford describes her, 'a terrible part which it is almost impossible to make interesting'.

Celia, Rosalind's friend and cousin in *As You Like It*, is a very different matter. Were Rosalind not given so many verbal fireworks, Celia would stand out well on her own account, for she too is witty, warm and highly intelligent. It is Celia who has insisted that Rosalind not only stay on at Court as her companion after her father has displaced and banished Rosalind's father, but that she is treated well and given the respect to which she is entitled. At the beginning we find her trying to jolly Rosalind along, telling her that had their positions been reversed she— Celia—would have taken comfort and happiness in the fact that the love and friendship between the cousins remained constant, and that they suffered together. More to the point, she emphasizes that she is her father's only child, and that there is unlikely to be any other heir, so that when the usurped lands come to her she will immediately hand over her illegal inheritance to Rosalind, the rightful heiress.

When Celia's father turns on Rosalind and banishes her on pain of death, Celia first stands up to him. 'If she be a traitor', she tells him, 'why so am I.' You are a fool, he tells her, Rosalind is just waiting her chance to take away from you everything I've given you: 'she is banished.'

> Pronounce that sentence then on me, my liege:
> I cannot live out of her company,

says Celia.

Celia does not hesitate to accompany her cousin to the Forest of Arden to look for Rosalind's father. She is the staunchest of friends, an example of Shakespeare's ability to write about good women when he wanted to, without making them nonentities.

As Agnes Latham says in her introduction to the Arden edition, 'Celia, like Adam, also wins her right of entry' [into Arden] by unselfishness and loyalty. Once in the forest she has the important function which only she can perform of displaying Rosalind in her double character of pretended boy and true girl. Her pulling of her cousin's feathers is one way in which the boy–girl cockiness is muted into something acceptable in a woman. Celia can make the retorts Orlando cannot and is the one person whom Rosalind does not command. When she wins Oliver we must assume she has won a prize. She has earned one.'

Janet Suzman, whom one might imagine to prefer Rosalind, has played Celia, and retains much affection for her. 'Celia is a most remarkable little animal. It's a wonderful part which I think is most underrated because it is in fact startlingly well written and funny. She's such a close-fisted little creature. She does not say a word more than she has to. She never opens her mouth unless she has something to say but when she does then it's right to the point.

'Once again the part shows a terrific friendship between women, genuine loyalty and faithfulness. Throughout the opening scenes of the play, Celia makes all the running—if you are banished then I'll be banished too. She may wilt a little later on, once the running has been taken over by Rosalind, but that splendid loyalty and friendship never falters for a moment. She seems to be waiting to fall in love too, and when she finally does is as pleased as her friend. But their natures are markedly different. Love makes Rosalind loquacious; it renders her friend Celia quite speechless.'

The Merchant of Venice provides two lesser roles for young women, Nerissa and Jessica. Both are independent and lively. Nerissa is described as Portia's waiting maid, but she is obviously a good deal more than that, as she is taken continually into Portia's confidence and she is not above a rebuke when she thinks it timely.

Portia's opening words are 'By my troth, Nerissa, my little body is aweary of this great world', to which Nerissa replies, 'You would be, sweet madam, if your miseries were in the same abundance as your good fortunes are.' This hardly argues a true mistress/servant relationship. It is Nerissa who also dresses up as a boy and accompanies her mistress to the court, disguised as the lawyer's 'clerk', and she joins in the fun with Portia and like her claims her betrothal ring from her lover in the guise of the boy in order to tease him with its loss at the end of the play. Nerissa must have been very much like the kind of lively girls who waited on the Queen at Court, and whom Shakespeare would have known.

Jessica is a different matter. She is Shylock's daughter, and, as a sub-plot to the bargain with Antonio and the pound of flesh—and, indeed, to the casket wooing—she steals Shylock's wealth and elopes with her Christian lover, Lorenzo.

Dover Wilson disliked her so much one feels he would have considered her in the same category as Goneril and Regan. 'Jessica', he wrote, 'is bad and disloyal, unfilial and a thief, frivolous, greedy, without any more conscience than a cat and without even a cat's redeeming love of home. Quite without heart, pilfering to be carnal, she betrays her father to be a light-of-lucre, carefully weighted with her sire's ducats.'

John Russell Brown asks if she is a minx who heartlessly runs away, the unfilial daughter of a persecuted Jew, or is she a princess held captive by an ogre?

Because nowadays we feel so much sympathy for Shylock, so have we lost sympathy for his unloving daughter. Says Robert Speaight: 'Jessica, by marrying Lorenzo and robbing her father into the bargain, breaks the barriers of history. An Elizabethan audience would have taken the point more kindly than we do.' One feels that Shakespeare probably did feel 'kindly' towards her, for he gives her and Lorenzo the most beautiful, lyrical lines in the play. Says Lorenzo:

> The moon shines bright! In such a night as this
> When the sweet wind did gently kiss the trees,
> And they did make no noise; in such a night,
> Troilus, methinks, mounted the Trojan walls,
> And sigh'd his soul toward the Grecian tents,
> Where Cressid lay that night.

and then he and Jessica vie with each other in line after lovely line, about lovers of old, ending with Lorenzo's speech

> Look how the floor of heaven
> Is thick inlaid with patines of bright gold.

Maybe, after all, these two not wholly admirable characters are merely coquetting, and thus the reference to Cressida is a deliberate one, but even if this is so Jessica deserves her place in the play if for no other reason than the poetry of that scene.

Olivia in *Twelfth Night* is different again from the other women in this chapter. There are divisions of opinion as to how old she is. In recent productions she has tended to be played as a younger woman than in the past, and this makes more sense of her subsequent marriage to Sebastian—exactly the same age as Viola —and of her attitude at the beginning of the play.

It is unlikely that she would have been the middle-aged frustrated spinster presented in some nineteenth-century productions. This would make nonsense of the fact that she is supposed to be so nubile and attractive that Orsino is besotted with her, that even Sir Andrew Aguecheek thinks he is in with a chance, and that deep down inside Malvolio lurks a consuming passion for her which is guessed at by Maria and which brings about his downfall.

She is certainly used to being in a position of authority. She is in command of her own household—almost a Court in miniature, with its relations, hangers-on, hierarchy of servants and its Fool. Underlying all the emotion that is going on, one is aware of the comings and goings of people about their household duties, the making of meals, the reality behind the dream.

John Masefield said of Olivia, 'Olivia is in an unreal mood of mourning for her brother. Grief is a destroying passion. Olivia makes it a form of self-indulgence, or one sweet the more to attract flies to her.' I have not seen that latter point made in any recent production of the play, but it is an interesting one. Would Orsino, one wonders, have been so desperate had he not always been presented with an adamant, weeping lady swathed in black veils?

John Russell Brown feels that Olivia 'can be seen to be of different ages—either mature years or extreme youth; and she can be melancholy or gay. And yet another Olivia might be suggested by the text: a very young girl, at first afraid of meeting the world and therefore living in a fantasy of seven-year mourning; then a girl solemnly repeating old saws with a new understanding of their truth ... and forgetting her discreet bearing in breathless eagerness.'

Looking at Olivia from a woman's point of view, I think she had probably had enough mourning by the time the play opens. She did not fancy Orsino, so it was useful to keep it up where he was concerned, but she was already getting restive and bored. She begins by exchanging repartee with the Fool, which suggests something more than a total submergence in grief, and the speed with which she falls, lock, stock and barrel, for Viola suggests she certainly must have been ready for something.

In the production by Terry Hands for the Royal Shakespeare Company in 1979 Olivia was, I feel, wrongly encouraged to play the whole role in a state of extravagant passion. Olivia believes herself to be in command, which is why her passion for Viola is so funny, and her great scene with Malvolio must be played straight. She must ask him out of genuine concern, thinking he must be ill, 'Wilt thou go to bed, Malvolio?', utterly unaware that these are words he has been waiting to hear from her for years and that Maria's forged letter has made him believe that this is just what she wants. Countless Malvolios have brought down the house from Shakespeare's day to our own, with his 'Ay, sweetheart, and I'll come to thee.'

Robert Speaight puts the whole tangle well. 'Orsino imagines he is in love with Olivia; Olivia imagines she is in love with Viola; Malvolio imagines he is in love with Olivia, and she with him. The play is a drama of discovery. Orsino discovers that he is really in love with Viola, whose assumed masculinity elicits his own; Olivia discovers that Sebastian will do just as well as Viola, because all she really wants is a man so long as he is not Orsino; and Malvolio discovers that he is in love with no one but himself.'

'Thou met'st with things dying, I with things new born'

Towards the end of his canon of plays, Shakespeare created three very young heroines who are linked in many ways to each other. Marina (*Pericles*), Perdita (*The Winter's Tale*) and Miranda (*The Tempest*) are all new-born creatures at the commencement of each plot—although we only hear of Miranda's infancy, and are not shown it. All are the victims of tempests of jealousy, and of physical tempests too. The sound of the sea is constantly in the ears of both them and us. Marina and Miranda spend their early days tossed literally on the waves, and Perdita is abandoned on a bleak beach. All three travel towards a second birth, the discovery of who they in fact are, their place in their families and, most important, towards love.

The most single striking quality they possess is that they are truly innocent, which is not to be confused with ignorance. They positively shine with goodness, and it is Shakespeare's genius that they are never prissy, never dull. Marina and Perdita are exceptionally lively and independent girls with strong personalities. Even Miranda, who has been so sheltered, will stand up to the father she adores and who has been her whole world, when she falls in love with Ferdinand.

To begin with Marina and *Pericles*, one of Shakespeare's most difficult and in many ways least satisfactory plays. The original source seems to be John Gower's fourteenth-century *Confessio Amantis*. The name of Gower would have been familiar to Shakespeare—he was buried in Southwark Cathedral—and although the episodic tale takes place around the Mediterranean coast, he is the narrator providing the links to the story throughout. Two versions of the play appeared in Shakespeare's lifetime, and the first performance was probably in 1608. It is a play where much has obviously been lost, either in the copying or in the printing, and most authorities agree that hands other than Shakespeare's made up parts of it. It is a kind of pageant or chronicle, never more than a series of incidents with many of the characters remaining two-dimensional.

As Robert Speaight says, 'The *Pericles* Bankside looked to see comes to us through a mist which is sometimes impenetrable, and at other times clears away. Why so faulty a text was republished without correction and twice within the author's lifetime, remains a mystery.'

But whoever was responsible for writing parts of it, the character of Marina can only have come from the hand of the master. She is truly the child of the sea, for as her long-lost mother says at the end, 'she was yielded there'.

After a variety of adventures (which have already included shipwreck) Pericles, Prince of Tyre, has met and married Thaisa, daughter of the King of Pentapolis. The young couple set off to return to Tyre with Thaisa heavily pregnant.

The ship runs into a dreadful tempest in which Marina is born and we suppose her mother dies.

> A terrible childbed hast thou had, my dear,
> No light, no fire, the unfriendly elements
> Forgot thee utterly

mourns Pericles, and his wife's body is put in a chest and set afloat. The nurse brings him a baby. 'Here is a thing too young for such a place,' she tells him, and Pericles manages to reach the shore with the 'piece of his dead queen' and takes the child to Dionyza, wife of the Governor of Tarsus, whose life he had saved earlier in the story. He asks her to bring up Marina while he travels the world, an endlessly grief-stricken pilgrim. Marina grows up, Dionyza is jealous that she outshines her own daughter and so plans to have her murdered. The attempt is interrupted by pirates who seize Marina and take her away to be sold to the brothels of Mitylene. The rest of the play deals with Marina's stout-hearted and effective defence of her virginity while knocking the brothel and its inhabitants into order, the return of her father, the discovery that her mother did in fact survive the tempest and, finally, her marriage to Lysimachus.

She is a most likeable girl. Seldom can a heroine have hung on to her virginity with such tenacity, and much of the action manages to be both moving and amusing. She is never a forlorn creature. When she is dragged into the brothel the Bawd asks if she is a virgin. 'We doubt it not,' say the pirates grimly, who have had a try. She is beautiful, and the Bawd is delighted. She has her cried in the market place for her virginity: 'He that will give most shall have her first.'

The Bawd spells out to Marina what is expected of her: 'You must seem to do that fearfully which you commit willingly; to despise profit where you have most gain. To weep that you live as you do makes pity in your lovers: seldom but that pity begets you a good opinion and that opinion a profit.' To which Marina replies 'I understand you not.' The Bawd's servant, Boult, claims 'I have bargained for the joint', to which his mistress replies 'Thou mayest cut a morsel off the spit' and Marina prays to Diana.

Some weeks later Marina has driven them all to distraction. 'Fie, fie upon her!' says the Bawd, 'she is able to freeze the God Priapus and undo a whole generation! We must either get her ravished or be rid of her . . . she would make a puritan of the devil.'

Along comes the governor, Lysimachus, who we see as a good-hearted but sophisticated womanizer. Hearing Marina's virtues extolled, he merely says, 'Faith, she would serve after a long voyage at sea.' But he does actually try to talk to her, and is surprised to find such a gentle creature in such a place. He asks her how long she has been on the game. Since she can remember, she tells him. Perhaps she misunderstands his meaning, he says—she is, after all, in a house of ill repute, and is merely 'a creature for sale'.

Marina then comes out with a statement which is remarkably modern today. 'Do you know this place to be a house of such resort and will come into it?' she points out. 'I hear say you are of honourable parts and the Governor of this place.' Lysimachus is abashed, gives her gold, and leaves, although he is obviously very attracted.

The Bawd makes one last attempt, encouraging Boult to rape Marina and take away her tiresome virginity, and during this scene of near-rape we watch Marina talk her way into escape. She offers to make just as much money for them by other means. She is a fine sewer and weaver, and has a splendid voice. She will teach these things and make them rich if she can only be left alone. She pleads against rape, against Boult taking away the virginity for which she had fought so hard, and castigates him for his whole way of life. In answer to his bemused query as to what other kind of life he could lead she says:

> Do anything but this thou doest. Empty
> Old receptacles, or common sewers, of filth;
> Serve by indenture to the common hangman:
> Any of these ways are yet better than this;
> For what thou professest, a baboon, could he speak,
> Would own a name too dear.

When we next meet her her fame has spread far and wide and Lysimachus is in love with her. Enter Pericles, back from his travels. Thaisa is also discovered, having been washed ashore alive after all, and having lived as a recluse through the years, and all ends happily. Marina, we feel, truly deserves her happy ending.

Because of the difficulties with the text, *Pericles* is not a popular choice. The Royal Shakespeare Company has produced it on a handful of occasions, the last in 1979 when it received a quick-moving studio production. The Prospect Theatre Company toured it in the early seventies as a kind of musical with the brothel scenes done in drag—Harold Innocent was an amazing Bawd, all black suspenders and leather. But there is little record of who has played Marina over the years.

The Winter's Tale poses no such problems, for it is a beautiful piece of work. It was written in 1610/11, and Shakespeare took as his source a tale by his arch-enemy, Robert Greene, which was called *Pandosto*. Greene emphasized that his was a story of Time—how time brings both concealment and discovery, and eventually a desired ending. Shakespeare actually creates Time as a person, and also added to *Pandosto* a range of characters, not the least being that 'snapper-up of unconsidered trifles', the rogue Autolycus.

Perdita too, the young heroine of *The Winter's Tale*, only
narrowly escapes death as an infant. Her father, Leontes, becomes
obsessed with a totally unfounded and paranoid suspicion that his
wife, Hermione, is having an affair with his lifelong friend,
Polixenes, King of Bohemia. He convinces himself that the child his
wife is carrying is not his. He sends a messenger to the Oracle at
Delphi to discover the truth of the matter, but cannot wait for the
verdict, and imprisons Hermione. His queen gives birth to Perdita,
and Leontes is told that she has died. He gives the baby to
Antigonus, telling him to take it away and expose it. At this point
the messenger returns from Delphi. Hermione is declared
innocent, and Leontes told that he will die without an heir should
he not find his lost child. Whereupon his existing heir, a young
boy, dies of some unspecified cause.

Perdita meanwhile has been taken to the coast of Bohemia—
Shakespeare furnishing it with one for the purposes of his
narrative—and is left there when Antigonus runs into a bear
(providing the author's most famous stage direction 'Exit, pursued
by a bear.'). The bear kills Antigonus, and the baby is found by
some country folk—'thou met'st with things dying, I with things
new born', and she is brought up as a shepherdess. Growing
beautiful, she attracts the notice of Florizel, son of Polixenes, who
disguises himself to meet her. Her father discovers the liaison,
forbids it, and Florizel and Perdita fly to—who else but
Polixenes's old friend Leontes? Thus is Perdita discovered again by
her father, the 'statue' of Hermione—who has lived retired all this
time—is miraculously brought back to life, and again all ends
happily.

The contrast between the formal Court scenes of the first half of
the play and the beautiful Arcadian idyll of the second is well
marked. Perdita is a delight. She is loved and loving, she is the
queen of the shepherds' feast day, a true and natural princess; and
Shakespeare has given her some wonderful verse.

> Here's flowers for you:
> Hot lavender, mints, savory, marjoram,
> The marigold, that goes to bed with the sun
> And with him rises weeping . . .
>   daffodils

> That come before the swallow dares, and take
> The winds of March with beauty; violets dim
> But sweeter than the lids of Juno's eyes
> Or Cytherea's breath; pale primroses
> That die unmarried, ere they can behold
> Bright Phoebus in his strength; a malady
> Most incident to maids . . .

A lovely description, if idealized, is that of Sir Thomas Overbury published in 1616 in which he described a shepherdess who might be Perdita. 'So far from making herself beautiful by art, that one look of hers is able to put all face-physic out of countenance. Though she be not arrayed in the spoil of the silkworm, she is decked in innocency, a far better wearing. . . . The golden ears of corn fall and kiss her feet when she reaps them, as if they wished to be bound and led prisoners by the same hand that felled them.' And later, 'She dares go alone and unfold sheep in the night, and fears no manner of ill, because she does none.'

Speaking of *The Winter's Tale*, F. R. Leavis said: 'The personal drama is made to move upon a complexity of larger rhythms— birth, maturity, death, birth . . . the concrete presence of time in its rhythmic processes. . . . No doubt it might be truly said of Florizel and Perdita as it has been of Ferdinand and Miranda, that they are lovers seen by one who is himself beyond the age of love, but Florizel and Perdita are not merely two individual lovers; they are organic elements in the poetry and symbolism of the pastoral scene, and the pastoral scene is an organic part of the whole play.' Trevor Nunn, who directed a remarkable production of *The Winter's Tale* in 1969, says, 'In the late plays, grace is achieved through love. Leontes is in a destructive nightmare "performed" in "a wide gap of time". Spring breaks through the grip of winter, love returns, enabling Leontes to awake his faith and be redeemed.'

On the whole it has been the part of Hermione which has attracted the great actresses. Mrs Siddons played it in the late-1700s, Ellen Terry in 1906. In 1887 Mary Anderson doubled the roles of Perdita and Hermione, an idea which Trevor Nunn incorporated into his 1969 production, Judi Dench playing the mother/daughter role.

She had great reservations about the idea at first. 'I felt I was too old for Perdita and too young for Hermione and that I would manage neither properly,' she says. But she did. The formal stark setting of the first half emphasized the differences, and the scenes of Leontes's jealousy were seen in slow motion with disturbing lighting effects so that you felt you saw with his eyes. On the other hand, the scenes with the shepherds were bright with flowers and colour, with Perdita dressed like a Rossetti shepherdess with flowing hair and looped draperies, and crowned with flowers.

In the end Judi Dench trusted to the director. 'I believed entirely in what he was trying to do and we succeeded in many ways in making that difficult story credible. Although he worked incredibly hard on the play it did not *feel* like work. If I thought I could play the role six different ways he would convince me that I could do it a hundred ways—I felt like a bottomless well.'

John Barton's production in 1976 was a far more sombre affair, with much more emphasis on the myth of Persephone and the ending of winter in a bleak, cold land. It was well done, but for many of those who saw the Nunn production in 1969 the scenes with Perdita remain for ever wrapped in a golden glow.

When we come to Miranda and *The Tempest* we have a somewhat different creature. Marina and Perdita had lived in the world, even if it was not the world into which either of them had been born. Perdita, in fact, had known nothing but love from her adopted parents, and had never doubted her origins until she was told differently. Marina was aware of something different, trying to remember what she could not possibly have done. 'Is this the wind westerly that blows?' she asks unsuspectingly of her intended murderer. 'South west,' he replies. 'When I was born the wind was north' she tells him.

Miranda has grown up totally isolated from all human beings except her father, Prospero. At the beginning of the play she is grown up and it is during the tempest from which the play takes its title that her father tells her of her origins, how he was displaced by his jealous brother and how he and the baby Miranda were put in a rotten boat and sent out to sea to drown. But they were washed on to the shores of a magic island, to which same island, driven by the tempest roused by Prospero's magic, is coming that very same brother, his son and his fellow-conspirators.

The Tempest was written about 1611, and although there is argument over whether it or *Henry VIII* was Shakespeare's last play it seems certainly to be the last play he wrote entirely himself.

It is an exceedingly difficult play to bring off because it is really one magnificent piece of poetry, a fitting summation of the rest of Shakespeare's work. It is also full of unanswered questions. The plot appears to have been devised by Shakespeare himself from folk lore in general currency and would almost certainly have been suggested to him by a similar event which actually happened in 1609. A fleet sailing to Virginia with 500 colonists found itself in the middle of a tempest. The *Sea Adventure*, the ship carrying the leaders of the expedition, was separated from the rest, and it was assumed it had been wrecked, but in fact the ship had gone aground in Bermuda. The island, like Prospero's, was alleged to be magic and full of voices, but the shipwrecked sailors found it a veritable paradise and were able to repair their ship and sail away.

Miranda is totally ignorant of the outside world, and has been enwrapped and protected by her father. The only shadow in the island paradise has been the attack made on her by the strange half-human creature Caliban. Caliban, Ariel—the spirit of air—and her father are all she has ever known.

When Ferdinand, the son of Prospero's wicked brother, arrives on the island Prospero deliberately encourages Miranda's interest in him, and at the same time treats him badly and so arouses her pity. She is torn between the father she has always worshipped and her growing love for Ferdinand. Both think the other divine when they first set eyes on each other.

> What is't? a spirit?
> Lord, how it looks about. Believe me, sir
> It carries a brave form.

and

> I might call him
> A thing divine; for nothing natural
> I ever saw so noble.

Ferdinand is equally amazed:

> Most sure, the goddess
> Of whom these airs attend! Vouchsafe my prayer
> May know, if you remain upon this island;
> And that you will some good instruction give
> How I may bear me here: my prime request
> Which I do last pronounce, is, O you wonder!
> If you be maid or no

To which Miranda replies

> No wonder, sir;
> But certainly a maid.

Prospero watches his daughter's growing involvement with Ferdinand, how she helps him carry wood and weeps tears over his torment. Finally he promises them that they will be joined in marriage, even calling down three goddesses, Juno, Ceres and Iris, to bless their betrothal. However, Ferdinand is solemnly warned about what will happen if he attemps to bed Miranda before marriage:

> If thou dost break her virgin knot before
> All sanctimonious ceremonies may
> With full and holy rite be minister'd,
> No sweet aspersion shall the heavens let fall
> To make this contract grow; but barren hate,
> Sour-eyed disdain, and discord, shall bestrew
> The union of your bed with weeds so loathly,
> That you shall hate it both.

Prospero makes himself known to his brother, who has been on another part of the island, releases Ariel, and prepares to return home after breaking his magic staff and abjuring his 'rough magic' in one of the most magnificent speeches Shakespeare ever wrote.

But unlike Marina and Perdita one is left wondering just how happy Miranda will be, so shielded has she been from reality. Seeing her father's wicked brother and the conspiring nobles, she utters the famous lines:

> How beauteous mankind is! O brave new world
> That hath such people in't!

To which Prospero answers drily, ' 'Tis new to thee . . .'

The Tempest was first given at Hallowmass, 1611, and it appears to have been revived in February 1613 as a celebratory piece on the betrothal of the young Princess Elizabeth to the Elector Palatine, after which it virtually dropped out of the repertoire. Sir William D'Avenant—he who rewrote *Macbeth*—produced his own version in 1667. This included a sister for Caliban, a girl-friend for Ariel and a twin for Miranda, and it was, said Charles Lamb, 'a vile mixture'. At the end of the eighteenth century a Mr F. G. Waldron wrote a sequel to it in which Prospero faces a rebellion on the way home and somehow retrieves his magic staff. But primarily it seems to have been remembered for its pageantry, and the special effects of the Masques of the Goddesses.

Miranda is a charming role, but has nothing like the meat for an actress of the other two. It is usually given to a pretty *ingénue*. Prospero remains a tremendous acting challenge for a man, and although I have seen a number of actors attempt it—Sir John Gielgud, Ian Richardson, Paul Scofield among them—it appears to remain virtually unplayable in a way which makes it truly consistent and believable.

'Making the mother, wife and child to see the son, the husband and the father tearing his country's bowels out ...'

With only a couple of exceptions, women in Shakespeare's historical dramas play very subordinate roles, whether in the Roman plays or in the lengthy British cycle which begins, historically, with *King John*, continues with *Richard II, Henry IV* 1 and 2 and *Henry V*, follows the history of the Wars of the Roses and ends with *Henry VIII*.

To begin with the Roman plays, Shakespeare went to Plutarch as his source for both *Coriolanus* and *Julius Caesar*, as he did for *Antony and Cleopatra*. It is hardly surprising, therefore, that women play such an insignificant part—with the exception of Volumnia. A Roman woman could be married from twelve years of age onward, could be divorced but could not divorce her husband, had no political rights, could not even leave her home without her husband's permission (and then only with a chaperone) and was supposed to be forbidden to drink wine on pain of death—a sentence which could be carried out by her family. Her influence, if she was strong-minded, could be shown only through her husband. Cato remarked, 'All nations rule their wives, we rule all nations, but our wives rule us. ...' This was Plutarch's world.

Brutus' wife, Portia, and Caesar's wife, Calpurnia, in *Julius Caesar* are classic vignettes of the Roman wife. Portia is clever—she was Cato's daughter—and brave—she wounds herself to prove to Brutus she can keep silent. She is noble and faithful, but Brutus does not immediately take her into his confidence. We only hear of her once again, towards the end of the play, when she has 'swallowed fire'—presumably poison—as she realizes Brutus will be defeated.

In Calpurnia, Shakespeare shows cleverly a more realistic aspect of most women—their intuition and even foreknowledge of events which has nothing to do with logic. Calpurnia is sure harm will come to Caesar if he goes that day to the Capitol, but she has no reason to give him. Almost she persuades him, but the conspirators play on his vanity. He turns against her advice, and the wheel of tragedy is set in motion.

Octavia in *Antony and Cleopatra* is made to seem a pleasant lady. One feels Antony might have settled down reasonably happily with the young widow had there not been such monumentally attractive opposition. Not surprisingly, Mrs Jameson approved of Octavia. 'The character of Octavia is merely indicated in a few touches but every stroke tells. We see her with downcast eyes, sedate and sweet, and looks demure with modest tenderness, dignified submission, the very antipodes of her rival!'

This sounds almost too sickly for a lady who in real life seems to have been quite a strong character, but Mrs Jameson does mention that she was quite remarkable: 'She received into her house the children of Antony and Cleopatra with her own, treated them with true maternal tenderness and married them nobly' (although historically they did not long survive after her own death).

The other women in the play, Iras and Charmian, are imaginary characters, waiting-maids of Cleopatra, but even in these two tiny roles we see a development of character from giggling waiting-women to true dignity at the end of the play. Both are given wonderful lines. It is Iras who says 'The bright day is done, and we are for the dark' and Charmian who gives the epitaph over the 'lass unparallel'd'.

Only Volumnia in *Coriolanus* has any real bearing on events and enough influence to change them. Coriolanus, having become disenchanted with the treatment he receives in Rome, has gone over to the enemy, the Volsci. When he is poised to sack the city his mother and wife and small son arrive to see him and it is his mother—every bit as proud and implacable as himself—who persuades him to change his mind. The play is in fact about the proud Coriolanus' three great battles—with Rome, with the Volsci and with his mother. It his mother who defeats him. She is strongly contrasted with his gentle, timid wife, who not for nothing does he address as 'my gracious silence'.

The two women are contrasted for us at the beginning of the play, sitting and sewing. The wife, Virgilia, is worrying about the safety of Coriolanus in battle, while his mother tells her firmly that she ought to prefer having her husband win honour on the field to making love to her in her bed. Meanwhile the boy is showing himself a chip off the old block by tearing the wings off butterflies.

Ellen Terry had a soft spot for Virgilia. She said: 'The majority of them [Shakespeare's women] are of strong character, high-mettled, quick-witted, resourceful. But Shakespeare's predilection for them did not prevent him from drawing with equal skill women of a different temperament. There is no play which provides us with a better proof of this than *Coriolanus*. Coriolanus' timid and sensitive wife, Virgilia, filled with terror for his safety every time he goes into action, is as masterly a creation as his lion-hearted, patriotic mother, Volumnia.'

John Wain points out that Volumnia is obviously a character on whom Shakespeare expended much thought, as she is hardly mentioned in Plutarch. She is as anti-democratic and contemptuous of 'the people' as her son but she is far more realistic, and can warn the latter to hide his feelings. 'Obviously Volumnia is not intended as a likeable woman. She is as tough and ruthless as her son; but she is, in the play's most important scene, made the mouthpiece of a power so sacred that even Coriolanus bows to it, and in doing so, redeems himself. And indeed Volumnia's haughtiness is necessary to the play's full effect. If she were a gentle, tender-hearted woman her plea to Coriolanus would have to be more softly phrased and accompanied by tears . . . it is the very memorable dignity of her appeal that makes it impossible for him to resist.'

It is a role favoured by 'grand' actresses, and a review from a *Times* critic of a performance by Sybil Thorndike shows why. 'In the supplication scene Dame Sybil stood for eternal Rome. When she began the lines

This fellow had a Volscian to his mother;
His wife is in Corioli, and his child like him by chance

her voice struck with a cutting edge of inspired bronze. Here was the classic tragedienne. Dame Sybil's voice had a defiant certainty; we knew Rome was behind her. She spoke for the centuries.'

As Speaight says, 'Volumnia appeals to his head in vain; only when she appeals to his heart will she gain a Pyrrhic victory, losing her son with the plea that saves the city.'

The women who flit briefly in and out of the pages of the English histories are certainly there to watch sons, husbands and fathers tearing their country's bowels out. Only two Queens, Margaret in the three parts of *Henry VI* and Katharine in *Henry VIII*, have large parts to play.

However, before we look at royalty there are three other women who have definite personalities of their own. The Duchess of York in *Richard II* is very human, and one of Shakespeare's realists. Her son is discovered plotting treason against the newly crowned Henry IV to try and put Richard II back on the throne. The Duke of York, discovering his son's treason (although he himself has only recently changed sides), rushes off to tell Henry IV, even if it means the death of his son.

Not surprisingly, the Duchess is not having any of that. As he tries to tell the King we hear the Duchess, who has ridden frenziedly after him, roaring, screaming and battering on the door to be let in. In spite of her husband's insults—'thou frantic woman'—she falls on her knees and will not get up until the King has pardoned her son in advance without even knowing what he is pardoning him for. Henry's efforts to make his aunt stand up, and her refusal to do so until the pardon has been given, provide the one scene of comic relief in a tragic play.

Young Lady Percy too in the first part of *Henry IV* is very much a person in her own right. She is obviously attractive, high-spirited and witty, with something about her of her namesake, Kate, of *The Taming of the Shrew*. When *her* husband, Hotspur, refuses to tell her what he is plotting she does not give herself a wound and suffer nobly like the Roman Portia; she clouts him round the head and tries to twist his little finger off to make him tell. In their scenes together, though so brief, we see a very real affection between Kate and Hotspur, and we can see enough in Kate to know that she could have sustained a longer role in another play.

Probably the strangest woman of all to appear in the histories is Shakespeare's version of Joan of Arc in *Henry VI* Part 1. This was partly because he was following the propaganda of his time, but also partly, one feels, because although the play comes chronologically towards the end of the cycle, it was the play he wrote first, when he was still very much learning his trade.

This Joan could hardly be more different than that of Shaw. She is not only shown as a genuine witch, she is also a whore and carrying a child whose father could be one of half a dozen. Robert Speaight says of this Joan: 'Shakespeare must not be held primarily responsible for the caricature of Joan. As a good Protestant Hall [Shakespeare's source] did not believe in divine locutions; witchcraft was a better explanation. And as a good patriot he could not be expected to agree that the French had the right to expel the English from territory that did not belong to them.'

The American writer Arthur Fiedler seeks mostly to fit Shakespeare around his own theories, but he has a point in his long chapter on Joan when he says that it is quite possible that Shakespeare himself truly believed that Joan was a witch, and there is a theory that she did herself—she certainly practised old rituals alongside Christianity.

John Wain describes the problem of Joan best, pointing out that Shakespeare himself may well have been ambivalent towards her: 'Joan is a witch. She derives her powers from the forces of hell. This power, in the early stages, is used to humble the English army, and consequently Shakespeare's attitude to her—on the surface— is one of simple enmity. But she is also a peasant girl, with a sharp tongue and a simple, direct attitude towards the overblown nobility with whom she has to co-operate. The result is a tug of war in which Shakespeare fails to arbitrate. We have to accept that Joan is evil; the alliance of political misrule with witchcraft looks forward to *Macbeth* and no doubt comes very much from the centre of Shakespeare's interests. But whenever she appears on the stage, we lean forward eagerly, anticipating a few minutes relief from the surrounding boredom and barbarism. She has not only the mystagogue's scorn of the dreary routines of practical men but also the peasant's dislike of fancy talk and high flown titles. . . .

'Joan of Arc disappears in the direction of the stake and the faggots before the end of Part I. Shakespeare, no doubt, felt embarrassed in the presence of a character about whom he could not clarify his own feelings. . . . His art is not yet ready for psychological realism and to make Joan three-dimensional would have called for psychological realism in plenty.'

So to the royalty. Apart from Queen Margaret, none of the royal ladies portrayed in Shakespeare was able to influence events, and even in her case the effect was marginal. As Janet Suzman says of the royal ladies, 'Only Cleopatra among his royal women had real political power with which to play, the actuality of power. The others are appendages to Kings and Princes. Margaret might move the bands of power about and make life more difficult for the body politic but she does not have the real power to force the men to behave differently. The women in the histories are the life-givers—they are there to produce heirs. There is a slight difference in Richard III—he woos both Anne and Elizabeth and twists them both round his finger, twice in the same play, with part flattery, part threats and the rest all sex.'

Looking at the plays in their historical sequence, rather than the order in which they were written, the first would be *King John*. This is one of Shakespeare's most flawed plays, with dates given for its writing from 1590 to 1598 inclusive. If it was based on a play on the same subject, *The Troublesome Reign*, published in 1591, then it is likely it came midway through the 1590s but there is a theory that it predated the anonymously written play, which would make it one of Shakespeare's earliest works.

King John had been portrayed in many ways, as a Protestant hero defying the Pope and as a ruthless monster, defeated by the Barons at Runnymede. Shakespeare came down more or less on the lines of 'King John was not a good man', and he particularly picked out the story of his treatment of Arthur as one of the main threads of the play. Arthur was John's nephew, son of his brother Geoffrey who has died. Constance, Arthur's mother, is extremely ambitious for her son, and it is her overweening neurosis which drives him into a head-on collision with John.

Mrs Jameson said of Constance that 'she was a mere instrument in the hands of others in spite of her fearless and determined spirit', but, she went on, she shows a 'total want of self control'. The other royal lady in the play, Queen Elinor, is also proud and ambitious, Margaret shown on a smaller scale.

John finally sees Arthur as a threat and persuades his Chamberlain, Hubert, to kill the boy. Hubert, however, proposes to put out the boy's eyes (for reasons never made plain), but is moved by him and decides to let him go. Arthur, though, mistrusts his change of heart and leaps from the castle wall to try to escape, only to kill himself on the rocks below.

Constance had already foreseen his death when he was taken from her, and Shakespeare gives her a most moving speech. His own eleven-year-old son, Hamnet, had died in the August of 1596 and was buried on the 11th. It has been thought that the play may have been written that year, and that Constance's words mirror Shakespeare's own loss:

> Grief fills the room up of my absent child
> Lies in his bed, walks up and down with me,
> Puts on his pretty looks, repeats his words
> Remembers me of all his gracious parts,
> Stuffs out his vacant garments with his form ...

and later

> I have heard you say
> That we shall see and know our friends in heaven:
> If that be true, I shall see my boy again.

It would seem likely that Shakespeare was trying to comfort himself.

Richard II's Queen appears only very briefly. Her only important scene is where she hears the gardeners discussing England using the metaphors of a garden and the need to clean it up 'when our sea-walled garden, the whole land, is full of weeds'. While she is watching them news comes to her of Richard's capture by Bolingbroke, and she curses the gardeners that their plants may not grow. Although the three villains, Bushy, Bagot and Green, are said in the play to have turned Richard's affections from his Queen (with an underlying homosexual innuendo), when Shakespeare shows the King and Queen together he shows only a devoted couple.

Henry IV has no Queen in the play; presumably Mrs Bolingbroke died before he came to the throne. . . . The next royal lady is Princess Katharine in *Henry V*. Again there is not much one can say about her, she is the necessary pawn in a royal marriage, but Shakespeare does give her the delightful scene with her woman, when she is trying to learn English, and the charming wooing scene at the end of the play. In real life she appears to have been quite tough, and her union with an officer of her household, Owen Tudor, founded the dynasty of that name. In the Royal Shakespeare's touring production of *Henry V*, with Michael Williams as the King, Polly James doubled the roles of Katharine and Bardolph's boy (the reverse of the Elizabethan casting), and it worked very well indeed, Dame Peggy Ashcroft going so far as to say that it was the most enchanting Katharine she had ever seen.

So then to Margaret, the one truly big royal role, which takes much of the centre of the stage throughout the three parts of *Henry VI*, and reappears in *Richard III*.

The three parts of *Henry VI* were possibly written about 1590, and were Shakespeare's first plays. Certainly it seems other hands had a part in them, especially in Part I, but there is enough of Shakespeare himself to be seen throughout the cycle. Margaret appears in the first part as a young woman, coming from France to marry the young, weak and religious-minded Henry. There is nothing of the hero of Agincourt in his son, and when the play opens the country has been torn to pieces for years, ever since Henry V died when his son was a baby. This would no doubt bring back memories to some of those who saw it, and who in their old age could remember the last time a powerful King had died and left a child on the throne, Edward VI, and the troubles that ensued.

There is nothing in common between the monk-like King and the sexy, politically minded Margaret, who becomes increasingly ruthless and obsessive as the Yorkists and Lancastrians drag out their endless wars. Her only true affection is reserved for her lover, Suffolk, who dies at the hands of her enemies. By the time

the third play is reached she can be rightly described as having 'a
tiger's heart wrapp'd in a woman's hide . . .'

As Robert Speaight says: 'Margaret has grown from her girlish
beginnings in Part I into a figure of ferocious strength. The scene in
which she mocks the captured York with a paper crown and a
napkin stained with the blood of his son, Rutland, excels in
dramatic intensity anything else in the first three plays of the
tetralogy.' Her words are vicious:

> Where are your mess of sons to back you now?
> The wanton Edward, and the lusty George?
> And where's that valiant crook-back prodigy,
> Dicky, your boy, that with his grumbling voice.
> Was wont to cheer his dad in mutinies?
> Or, with the rest, where is your darling Rutland?

Not surprisingly, the three parts of *Henry VI* are performed only
rarely, and certainly one of the most successful attempts was Peter
Hall and John Barton's adaptation under the name of *The Wars of
the Roses* in 1963, in which Dame Peggy Ashcroft played Margaret.

T. C. Worsley said of her: 'In the first play she is the wanton
Queen, already despising the saintly King she has married and we
see her already as a woman of boundless ambition and toughness of
will, as relentless as any of the men. Among many superb moments
she has given us in the theatre I shall long remember the speech she
makes to her dispirited followers making their last stand. She
summons up some inner strength from out of the weariness of
defeat and although she speaks like a lioness, the heart you feel is
already dead.'

Dame Peggy herself says 'one of the parts which has fascinated
me most is Margaret of Anjou', giving as part of the reason the fact
that she combines Shakespeare's ability to portray both girls and
older women. 'The *Henry VIs* are, of course, very early plays and I
found it fascinating to discover right at the beginning, when
Margaret is about eighteen, a scene which is very reminiscent of
The Taming of the Shrew—which he wrote next. And yet there is not
another character who approaches the tragic-poetic quality of
Margaret in the scene where she says farewell to Suffolk until you
get to Cleopatra.

'Those two plays were very much in my mind when I was playing it because she is as ruthless and relentless as Cleopatra—although not, of course, as subtle. It was our intention in those three plays, and we used to discuss it with Peter Hall, to present an epic because it is the sweep of the story and the history in the plays, rather than the minute characterizations, which are important. The characters are delineated in very simple terms, not with great subtleties, although they are very magnificent nevertheless.

'Margaret is certainly one of the most fascinating and demanding characters in them—although she is a sort of monster. I think that Margaret's bestiality and brutality to York is the result of the murder of Suffolk and especially the decapitation of Suffolk. Why else does Shakespeare end Part I with Margaret cradling the head of her lover in her arms? Everyone is under a curse in that play. Margaret is a truly tragic character because in her overriding desire for power and domination are the seeds of her tragedy and you see how she is, in a sense, punished at the end when she loses her own son who she loves the most after she loses Suffolk. Whether she cares about the loss of Henry is, of course, another matter, but it is finally the death of her son that drives her mad and then she embodies the curse in *Richard III*, although as a point of historical fact she had gone back to France before the period covered by *Richard III*.

'I found it fascinating to see a recent production of all three parts in full, to see the scenes we cut in *The Wars of the Roses*. I think the plays can be cut, though, because they are not major works and there is a lot of repetition in the battle scenes—but they are very splendid early stuff.'

Later historians have given a different character altogether to Richard III, but there is no point in reading our present knowledge into Shakespeare's portrait. Historically accurate or not, he is what he is, and it has been said that in order to understand him we need to have been introduced to the psychotic youth he is in *Henry VI*. In reality, too, he appears to have been devoted to his wife and she to him, but to show yet another nasty aspect of Richard, Shakespeare makes his wooing of Lady Anne a calculated piece of sadistic pleasantry.

To give it an extra frisson, it takes place across the coffin of her murdered father-in-law. In her one short scene with Richard she sees him, rails at him, spits on him, then falls into his arms like a ripe plum. Jan Kott says of her 'Anne does not give herself to Richard out of fear. She will follow him to reach rockbottom . . . to prove to herself that all the world's laws have ceased to exist. Lady Anne goes into Richard's bed to be destroyed.' One imagines Shakespeare put in the scene for its dramatic impact, but it is good enough to tempt actresses into what is a very tiny part. Ellen Terry merely says repressively of Anne that she is 'frankly a study in female weakness'.

The last of Shakespeare's Queens was very recent history, Katharine of Aragon in *Henry VIII*. To deal with the subject at all he had to tread on very delicate ground indeed, and it seems to be agreed that not all the writing in the play is Shakespeare's own.

The politics of the period are almost by-passed, there are no right or wrong factions in the play, merely tides of fortune. Anne Bullen's execution is never referred to, since the play ends with the triumphant christening of the little Elizabeth, and Cranmer's prophecy that 'This royal infant—Heaven still moves about her—though in her cradle, yet now promises upon this land a thousand, thousand blessings. . . .'

Yet although Katharine is deposed to make way for Anne, it is she and her arch-enemy Wolsey who have the best two roles in the play. In Katharine there are strong overtones of Hermione, but Katharine is drawn with a stronger brush. She may be wronged and falsely accused, but she never forgets for one moment that she is the daughter of kings and that her nephew, Charles V, is the most powerful man in Europe—and she lets nobody else forget it either. Yet she has generosity, even to Wolsey; saying when she hears of his death 'His faults lie gently on him!'

Ellen Terry observed of Katharine: 'It is said that Shakespeare had many collaborators in *Henry VIII* but I'll be sworn that Katharine is all his work. Who but Shakespeare could have shown in a few deft touches how the elements are mixed in this nature, pride and humility, rebelliousness and resignation, hardness and softness. Katharine is another example of Shakespeare's sensitiveness to racial characteristics. Surely she is as Spanish as Volumnia is Roman and Juliet Italian.'

'I must be patient till the heavens look with an aspect more favourable'

Shakespeare wrote about a number of women who had to put up with a great deal. Unjust accusations of unfaithfulness appear in several of the plays, and Hermione, in *The Winter's Tale*, and Imogen, in *Cymbeline*, both win through only after much suffering (although how each reacts to her accusation differs). Helena, in *All's Well That Ends Well*, is not accused of anything, but the entire play is devoted to her single-minded attempt to make sure the man of her choice marries her. Fashions change, and Helena used to be considered the epitome of the noble, suffering heroine—now she seems to be rather unpopular. I have also put Gertrude into this chapter, although she brought her troubles on herself, in part because it is difficult to place her anywhere. Actresses find her a hard task.

All the suffering ladies were highly admired by Mrs Jameson, as can be seen from her views on Hermione. 'The character of Hermione exhibits what is never found in the other sex and but rarely in our own—yet sometimes; dignity without pride, love without passion, tenderness without meekness. To conceive a character in which there enters so much of the negative required perhaps no rare and astonishing effort of genius, such as created a Juliet or a Lady Macbeth—but to delineate such a character in the poetical form, to develop it through the medium of action and dialogue, without the aid of description, to preserve its mild and serious beauty, its impassioned dignity and at the same time keep the strongest hold upon our sympathy and our imagination . . . it is this which renders the character of Hermione one of Shakespeare's masterpieces.'

When we first encounter Hermione at the beginning of the play she is a happily pregnant wife, already mother of a small boy. She has an obvious affection for her husband's friend, Polixenes, but nowhere is there any suggestion that this is anything more. We gradually become aware of Leontes's growing and irrational jealousy before she does, as Shakespeare gives him a number of speeches direct to the audience. In Trevor Nunn's 1969 Stratford production the feeling of growing madness was enhanced by the use of strange lighting during these asides while the rest of the cast acted out, in slow motion, what Leontes imagines he has seen. It was very effective.

The little boy, Mamillius, appears only briefly, as he is to die as a result of his father's jealousy, but he is beautifully observed. The scene with his mother and her women, where he is determined to tell them one of those interminable child's ghost stories which begin 'There was a man . . . Dwelt by a churchyard . . .' and so on, could well be a child of today retelling the plot of a horror film.

When Leontes finally turns on her and accuses her of adultery she roundly defends herself, but she is convinced that he does not know what he says, that his mind is deranged.

> There's some ill planet reigns:
> I must be patient till the heavens look
> With an aspect more favourable.

She is not, she says given to weeping as many of her sex are, but the fact that she does not, she tells him, does not mean that she is not moved.

> I have that honourable grief lodg'd here, which burns
> Worse than tears drown.

Leontes has her thrown into prison, although virtually his entire Court turns against him. In prison she gives birth to Perdita, and her confidante and friend, Paulina, decides that it would be best to tell the King she has died. She brings the baby to show him, and stands up to him roundly, abusing him in no uncertain terms— another of Shakespeare's brave and loyal friends—and forces him to look at the child.

> Behold, my lord,
> Although the print be little, the whole matter
> And copy of the father—eye, nose, lip,
> The trick of his frown, his forehead ...
> The very mould and frame of hand, nail, finger:
> And thou, good goddess Nature, which hast made it
> So like to him that got it, if thou hast
> The ordering of the mind too, 'mongst all the colours
> No yellow in't, lest she suspect, as he does,
> Her children not her husband's!

As Paulina says, it is the worse for it, in fact.

It is a splendid scene, which ends with Leontes demanding the child be taken away and slaughtered. We know what does happen—Perdita lives—but at this stage the first audiences must have believed that Hermione was dead, and that the baby would die likewise.

Hermione then vanishes from the play until the very end, where we learn that she has lived in seclusion for sixteen years. Leontes, who now knows the truth and has recovered from his terrible brainstorm, has spent the time lonely and grief-stricken, having lost wife and both children. Finally, when Perdita is restored Paulina takes him to see a perfect statue of Hermione. It is so lifelike that he embraces it, and finds, of course, that it is indeed Hermione.

Some writers have read a Christian redemption into the play, Hermione personifying faith and grace. 'It is required you do awake your faith,' she says when stepping down from the pedestal. But it seems to have more in it of the old myth of the rejuvenation of spring after winter. Northrop Frye says that while Hermione is continually associated with the word grace, 'such grace is not Christian or theological grace which is superior to the order of nature, but a secular analogy of Christian grace which is identical with nature. ... The symbolic reason for the sixteen-year gap is clearly to have the cycle of the year reinforced by the slower cycle of human generations.'

Trevor Nunn said that 'Leontes is in a destructive nightmare, "performed" in a "wide gap of time". Spring breaks through the grip of winter, love returns, enabling Leontes to awake his faith and be redeemed. Shakespeare absolves the gods of our failures; the responsibility is in us, the faith demanded is faith in ourselves.'

Helen Faucit played the role with Macready in 1837, and wrote of the final scene: 'Oh, can I ever forget Mr Macready at this point! At first he stood speechless, as if turned to stone; his face with an awe-struck look upon it. Could this, the very counterpart of his queen be a wondrous piece of mechanism? Could art so mock the life? He had seen her laid out as dead, the funeral obsequies performed over her, with her dear son beside her. Thus absorbed in wonder, he remained until Paulina said, "Nay, present your hand." Tremblingly he advanced, and touched gently the hand held out to him. Then what a cry came with, "O, she's warm!"

'It is impossible to describe Mr Macready here. He was Leontes very self. His passionate joy at finding Hermione really alive seemed beyond control. Now he was prostrate at her feet, then enfolding her in his arms. I had a slight veil or covering over my head and neck supposed to make the statue look older. This fell off in an instant. The hair which came unbound, and fell on my shoulders, was reverently kissed and caressed. The whole change was so sudden, so overwhelming, that I suppose I cried out hysterically, for he whispered to me, "Don't be frightened, my child! Don't be frightened! Control yourself!" All this went on during a tumult of applause that sounded like a storm of hail.'

So to Imogen and *Cymbeline*. Imogen too is falsely accused of adultery, but Shakespeare's keenest admirer could hardly describe *Cymbeline* as one of his great plays. Shaw dismissed it as 'stagey trash'. It is more than that, but it has its longueurs. It may have been written about 1610, possibly for the investiture of the Prince of Wales, as there are so many references to Wales and the Welsh, and part of the action takes place there. It has something of the episodic nature of *Pericles*, and for his sources Shakespeare used two very disparate tales—the so-called history of King Cymbeline in Holinshed and the 'Wager' story from Boccaccio's *Decameron*; an unlikely mix.

To try briefly to summarize the plot; Cymbeline is King of Britain, and is currently fighting the Romans. He has an only daughter, Imogen, and he has recently married again a woman who wants Imogen for her own son, Cloten, to secure his succession to the throne. Imogen had two brothers who disappeared mysteriously in infancy. Imogen, however, marries the man of her choice, Posthumus, who is then banished and finds his way to Rome. He is, one feels, a less than bright young man, and he brags nightly of the beauty and virtues of Imogen. Enter the lecherous Iachimo, who wagers him that he can seduce Imogen in one night and will bring back proof.

Iachimo duly turns up at Cymbeline's court and assails Imogen, who of course rejects him. However, he asks if he may leave a chest of treasure in her bedroom for safe-keeping and she agrees. This is a funny scene, and I have seen the lid raised on the evilly smiling faces of both Ian Richardson and Ben Kingsley in recent productions to a roar from the audience. Iachimo notes details of the bedroom—and, indeed, physical details of Imogen—and convinces Posthumus that he has seduced her.

Posthumus sends word to Britain to his servant to kill Imogen, and writes her a lying letter asking her to come to Milford Haven to meet him, to enable this to be done. When they get there and there is no Posthumus the servant tells all to Imogen and helps her escape, dressed as a boy. Events happen thick and fast after that. She meets two noble lads living in a cave (yes, they turn out to be her brothers); she feels ill and takes medicine given her in good faith by the servant which turns out to have been poisoned by the Queen; the lumpish Cloten turns up dressed in Posthumus's clothes and has his head cut off, his headless body being mistaken by Imogen for that of her husband. She is then swept up by the invading Romans, and all of them—including Posthumus, who has landed with them—finally arrive back at Cymbeline's court, where there is a kind of Keystone Kops last scene in which everybody explains bits of the action to everyone else, half the cast throw off their various disguises—including Imogen—and everybody lives happily ever after except the Queen, who dies.

In spite of its uneven writing there is some fine verse—'Fear no more the heat of the sun,' for example—and Imogen has some lovely lines. Robert Speaight feels that there is a definite point where the play takes off and that is when Imogen arrives at Milford Haven in answer to the false letter. There is her desire to get there—'O for a horse with wings!'—followed by her desolation when the servant, Pisanio, tells her of Posthumus's treachery;

> I see before me, man: not here, nor here,
> Nor what ensues but have a fog in them
> That I cannot look through.

'It is a marvellous passage,' says Speaight. 'Shakespeare, having fallen in love with Imogen, is himself again. In his mastery of a new prosody, he reminds one of a veteran jockey on a young filly taking Beecher's Brook in an easy leap, with the rest of the field left nowhere.'

Speaking of Hermione and Imogen—both parts which she had played—Ellen Terry said: 'Dignity under a false accusation and unwavering love in spite of it, were evidently greatly admired by Shakespeare for he exalts them in Hermione and again Imogen. I am "foolish fond" of this heroine. When I am asked which is my favourite part her name rises spontaneously to my lips.

'She enchants me so I can find no fault in her. Well, I am in good company. Two poets, Tennyson and Swinburne, love Imogen above all Shakespeare's women and Bernard Shaw says she is an enchanting person of the most delicate sensitiveness and of the highest breeding and courage, for she is made to suffer trial after trial. When I came to know her well—it was in 1896 at the Lyceum—I was able to understand how, after all the crimes her husband has committed against her—and the worst I think is his writing that lying love letter to bring her to Milford Haven within reach of his revenge—she can throw her arms round him and say in an ecstasy of tenderness "why did you throw your wedded lady from you?"

'That's just what an impulsive person *would* say and Imogen is impulsive above all things. Her impulses are always whole-hearted ones too—she never does things by halves.'

Judi Dench has also played both Hermione and Imogen. 'They are both really very strong women and that must be remembered all the time. Imogen is truly extraordinary. After all that's happened to her she then reads the letter and knows she is going to be killed when suddenly the servant, Pisanio, says I've got an idea which will take you near to Posthumus. She has broken down, has ordered him to follow Posthumus's orders and indeed kill her, then suddenly she bounces up again and decides to follow Pisanio's advice. She's a lady of great and rare spirit. I had a long letter from someone who saw the play when I was in it who said she found it extraordinary that Shakespeare should write this girl who is never brow-beaten, never gives in and who, whatever happens to her, springs back to life every time. She accepts every kind of challenge. I used to feel downbeat by the interval but the director, David Jones, said you mustn't feel that at all. She's defied everyone, including her father who is little better than a tyrant. She's a rebel and you must play her as such.'

Helena, in *All's Well That Ends Well*, is something of a rebel too, but no other women's role in Shakespeare has suffered such a change of opinion. Alone, Helena seems to have felt the shift caused by the changing place of women.

Nobody is sure when the play was written, although the date most often given is 1603, between *Troilus and Cressida* and *Measure for Measure*. It may even have been the second version of a play first called *Love's Labours Won*, mentioned in 1598, but in any event it does not seem to have ever been performed in Shakespeare's own lifetime.

Again Shakespeare used Boccaccio as a source, but the 'bed trick', where one girl is substituted for another, was commonplace in folk stories. It was to be used by Middleton in *The Changeling*— the play takes its title from it—and would be used again by Shakespeare in *Measure for Measure*. It had happened in real life in Shakespeare's time when a lady who wanted to sleep with the Earl of Oxford swapped places with his current mistress. Presumably it was not considered all that degrading in Shakespeare's own day.

Helena, then, when the story opens is a penniless orphan who has been brought up by the Countess of Rousillon—incidentally one of Shakespeare's best small parts for an older woman. She is madly in love with Bertram, the Countess's son, a match not possible because of her own poor birth. The King of France is very ill, and doctors have failed to cure him, so Helena, whose father was a physician, decides to try. She succeeds, and the King offers her anything she wants. She wants Bertram, and says so. He does not want her in the least, but is forced to marry her. On the wedding night he runs away, saying he will only live with her if she can come to him provably pregnant by him, which will never happen.

Nothing daunted, Helena sets off in pursuit. When she catches up with him he is busy trying to seduce Diana. Helena persuades Diana to change places with her—the bed switch—and Bertram duly sleeps with Helena (not recognizing her) and gets her pregnant. By the end of the play he has returned to France, having been told Helena is safely dead, and is about to marry yet another young lady when Helena and Diana arrive. Diana claims the right to his hand, saying he has seduced her. Bertram denies it, then Helena steps forward and all is revealed. We are then supposed to believe that everybody lives happily ever after.

Coleridge considered Helena Shakespeare's 'loveliest creation', and Mrs Jameson echoed the nineteenth-century view of her. 'There never was, perhaps, a more beautiful picture of a woman's love, cherished in secret, not self consuming but in silent languishment, not pining in thought, not passive and desponding over its idol—but patient, hopeful, strong in its own intensity and sustained by its own fond faith!' Though poor and lowly, continues Mrs Jameson, she shows true breeding and delicacy of feeling.

In his commentary on the play G. K. Hunter says that the dilemma is whether Helena is mean of spirit to stoop to such a trick or whether she is just a clever wench out of a simple folk tale. 'She is something of a schemer who must make her way in the new world of social mobility and opportunism.'

It is also a play about disparities of rank and how a virgin can actively pursue a matter of love without incurring dishonour. It is a symbol of the use of virginity and its transformation to a natural fertility. Helena claims Bertram not only by virtue of the symbolic ring but also by virtue of the child within her.

If Helena does not come out very well nowadays, Bertram—over whom all the energy is expended—seems hardly worth a rush, a spoiled, petulant and unpleasant young man who can switch from one girl to another without a thought. But he reacts to Helena's pursuit as most men would.

John Wain says Bertram's reaction to Helena is utterly convincing, 'brow-beaten by the King into marrying a girl he does not want. In a fairy tale Helena's motives would not be examined—of course the goose girl wants to marry the prince. But she claims her reward in the teeth of Bertram's horrified recoil. This is realism. The kind of girl who engineers a marriage for herself is not the kind to worry about whether her bridegroom loves her or not; once the ring is on her finger, she feels there will be plenty of time to bring him round to her point of view.'

I must admit my own favourite view of Helena was given in a lecture by Dr Henry Yellowlees, under the title 'Medicine and Surgery in Shakespeare's plays', in 1955. 'In my salad days I accepted the view that Bertram was a loathsome mixture of snob and cad, whose treatment of the lovely and virtuous Helena was truly contemptible. I hold it still, but I have come to realise that he was in some ways sinned against as well as sinning and that Helena, in spite of having many beautiful and pathetic things to say, is really an obnoxious young woman who merits, if women ever did, the classical title of "designing minx".

'For years I have mistrusted her but it was only when reading the play with this lecture in mind that I realized how thoroughly she is on the make from start to finish and how *very well* able she is to look after her own interests. She is the centre and focus of all the medical interest of the play; she is the perfectly drawn presentation of the unqualified practitioner—the Quack.'

Dr Yellowlees goes on, amusingly, to throw doubt on whether Helena could indeed have cured the King's fistula with any kind of medicine then known—although recognizing that perhaps magic enters into the story here. But returning to Helena he says, 'I may be wrong but I don't think Shakespeare's truly "loveliest creation" (Coleridge) would have opened a discussion on the keeping and losing of virginity with such a half bred bit of riff raff as Parolles.' Shakespeare, he feels, devises a suitable fate for his Quack; 'he marries her to Bertram'.

Perhaps the last word should be left with Ellen Terry. 'Both Helena and Julia (*Two Gentlemen of Verona*) belong to the doormat type. They bear any amount of humiliation from the men they love, seem almost to enjoy being maltreated and ignored by them.

They hunt them down in the most undignified way when they are trying to escape. The fraud with which Helena captures Bertram who has left his home and country to get away from her is really despicable.'

Hamlet seems to have been written in 1601, and for his sources Shakespeare may have drawn on Kyd's *The Spanish Tragedy*, perhaps on a lost play of *Hamlet* and almost certainly on Saxo Grammaticus. This play was acted at Newington Butts in 1594, and was still being performed in 1596. There is a reference to the ghost in it, 'which cried so miserably at the theatre, like an oyster-wife, "Hamlet, revenge!"'

Both the women in *Hamlet* appear somewhat spiritless creatures, and although Gertrude is usually ranked with the major Shakespearean roles, when you examine the text she has very little to either do or say apart from the great closet scene.

Barbara Jefford played Gertrude at the National Theatre to Albert Finney's Hamlet, and at the Old Vic with Derek Jacobi. 'I think it is a frightfully difficult part. I never have understood why people talk about it as one of the "great" women's roles. There is one good scene and that's it. You are not given any of the detail of the truly big roles—Lady Macbeth, Rosalind, Cleopatra, Viola. Gertrude is passive, you have to flesh her out in an extraordinary way to make her work between scenes. There are literally whole scenes where she just comes on and says a couple of things, usually nothing very much and then rather formal such as welcoming speeches to Rosencrantz and Guildenstern.

'When you play her you have to get a line on her to make it possible for her to *be* there and not say or do anything. She's been played as neurotic or even drunk. I didn't do either of those things but I've heard of it being done, playing her absolutely smashed right up to the end when she says "the drink, the drink", all working to it, which I think is silly. But there is not a lot to her, strangely enough.

'It is interesting trying to find reasons for her behaviour although I don't believe Shakespeare wrote her with many reasons. Did she know about the murder? *I* think she did, yes . . . I don't think you could live in an enclosed atmosphere like the

Danish Court and not know there was something very strange
about it. There is this very fit man lying in an orchard for an after-
dinner sleep and someone comes in and pours something in his ear
and he's dead. You've got to know—and who is the most obvious
person to have done it? The man who wants to be King. The
rumours must have been rife. It was a small community, even
smaller than a village and alive with intrigue and plots. She must
have known unless she was absolutely stupid, which I don't think
she is—she just behaves stupidly. I think she knows but doesn't
want to know, won't talk about it, won't recognize it, won't admit
it even to herself.

  'I think one of the main things about her is that she is a very sexy
lady who desperately needs it and finds Claudius very, very
attractive. The King is a noble character who's been away a lot
fighting wars and is probably rather boring and that isn't enough
for her. It's as simple as that. It *is* simple but it is very complicated
to show because there are no lines. She never says anything about
Claudius, never mentions him. The situation has arisen before the
play starts. There she is, married in indecent haste to the villain of
the piece.

  'Her best lines come in the scene over Ophelia's grave when
Hamlet returns, lines like

> as patient as the female dove,
> When that her golden couplets are disclos'd,
> His silence will sit drooping . . .

'Playing it twice near together was fascinating. In the National
Theatre production directed by Peter Hall, in the last scene of all
when she takes the poisoned cup from Hamlet she did so by
mistake, she truly didn't know. When I did it the next year at the
Old Vic directed by Toby Robertson I *knew* it was poisoned and
drank it knowing. I drank it because there was nothing more I
could do and also because I did not want him to drink it. I know
that was better than the other way I did it. It needed to have some
real intention behind it.

  'There is all that business with the pearl and you feel that
if Claudius has put something in the drink there must be some-

thing wrong with it since he hasn't demonstrated anything but wickedness all the way through the piece.

'One point Peter Hall and I worked out was the time in the play when Gertrude actually goes off Claudius and falls out of love with him. The veils are removed from her eyes after the closet scene when Hamlet has absolutely forced her to see what a wretched sort of life she's been leading and what an awful man he is. It is when Claudius comes on after that, having heard of the death of Polonius, and tries to carry on with their relationship that she finds she can't any more. It was shown as purely a visual thing—the lines are not there. But it made it logical that from then on she begins to feel really sick and that, in the end, leads on to the desire to die.'

'Our bright day is done and we are for the dark'

Juliet, Ophelia, Desdemona and Cordelia all die tragically before their time—Juliet and Ophelia by their own hands, Desdemona and Cordelia by murder.

Romeo and Juliet was written about 1595, some years before the sequence of great tragedies and when Shakespeare was still writing comedies and also the historical plays. Unlike the later tragedies, we feel that the tragedy in *Romeo and Juliet* comes about far more by misfortune and force of circumstance than because of a foredoomed series of actions. There is no feeling of that terrible wheel on which the characters in *Macbeth* find themselves trapped. Romeo and Juliet are truly star-cross'd, and their tragedy is brought about by events outside their control.

Shakespeare's source was a long poem by Arthur Broke called *Romeus and Juliet*, and he followed it fairly faithfully, but as in other examples of plays where Shakespeare has closely stuck to an existing source there are brilliant creations of his own—Mercutio is all Shakespeare.

Mrs Jameson rhapsodized over Juliet more than over any other of her heroines. 'All Shakespeare's women, being essentially women, either love or have loved or are capable of loving; but Juliet is love itself. Passion is her state of being and out of it she has no existence. It is the soul within her soul; the pulse within her heart; the life blood in her veins.

'The picture in *Twelfth Night* of the wan girl dying of love, who pined in thought and with a green and yellow melancholy, would never surely occur to us when we think of the enamoured and impassioned Juliet, in whose bosom love keeps a fiery vigil, kindling tenderness into enthusiasm, enthusiasm into passion and passion into heroism.'

Shakespeare makes Juliet barely fourteen, four years younger than Broke's original, and the overriding problem for any actress attempting the role is to blend Juliet's extreme youth with the experience and technique necessary to put over some of the most complex and marvellous verse he ever wrote. Certainly attempts to cast the part on looks alone, as in the Zeffirelli film version in 1968, do not work.

Ellen Terry despised 'the vulgar idea of Juliet—that the all-beautiful and heaven-gifted child is a lovesick girl in white satin'. She continues, saying that Shakespeare 'endowed Juliet, a very young girl, with the inward freedom which produces courage ... Her age may be one of the reasons for this. To us now, a girl of fourteen seems a mere child. There is any amount of evidence that in the days when the average span of human life was shorter, people arrived at maturity sooner. At fourteen they were not children but adults and Shakespeare's Juliet at fourteen is more mature than her years would make her today. There is some truth in the saying that an actress cannot play Juliet until she is too old to look like her. Whatever her age let her remember that Juliet is something more than a great lover—she is a great poet!

'She is fearless when she marries Romeo, fearless when he is banished and she has to face dangers and difficulties alone ... during the brief time between her marriage and her death, her situation is indeed terrible but it does not break her spirit.

'Juliet has to face considerable parental tyranny. In her extremity she appeals to her mother and her nurse for help. Both women have been shocked at Capulet's violence and have tried to calm him down but they have no notion of supporting Juliet against him.' Her reaction, continues Ellen Terry, is to assume a very humble and docile manner. 'She uses the weapon of duplicity very cleverly and her parents are completely taken in and defeated by it.'

Turning to the great 'potion speech' made by Juliet before she takes the drink which will counterfeit death, and in which she tells her fears of waking, surrounded by the truly dead, Ellen Terry says that 'an actress must be in a state of grace to make that speech hers. She must be on the summit of her art where alone complete abandonment to passion is possible'.

Dame Peggy Ashcroft has played Juliet three times. 'To talk about Shakespeare's heroines at all is taking on a formidable task. It covers such an enormous scope of ideas and feelings. I suppose the first thing that one thinks about—and it has always been a very debatable point—is that Shakespeare's heroines were written to be played by boys because boys played the parts at the time, and there is a tendency to think of them with that in mind.

'Up to a point it is true—that goes for the boy impersonators, the Rosalinds, Violas and Imogens, but being the colossal artist that he was he wrote really for girls and women. I always feel that the "heroines" as one calls them, *must* be girls. I think one has to bear in mind the age he conceived them as being because there has, in the past, been a tendency for actresses to play Portia and Rosalind, for example, when they were in middle age as middle-aged women. Unless—and it is perfectly possible—you can assume youth in middle age, I think youth is essential.

'But when we get to Juliet there is the ludicrous theory that you can only play Juliet when you are in your teens. I think it is nonsense because any actress who is capable of playing Juliet can preserve that quality of youth into her thirties. I played it when I was twenty-two, twenty-four and twenty-eight and strangely enough I met a couple of Americans on a boat and they were talking about it as they had just seen it. They said they had only seen it once before and it "was played by someone much older than you for the Oxford University Society" and I said well, it was me. . . . So you see that is what I mean, that youth is something you characterize, that you play.

'You know more about the essentials of youth when you are a bit beyond it than when you are in your teens. I remember that when I was in my teens I felt that I was about to play one of the great tragic roles of Shakespeare and therefore I had to play A Great Tragic Role which is quite the wrong way round. One has to imagine a girl of fourteen in the circumstances Juliet found herself in and that is the problem for any actress. She has to be fourteen, in those particular circumstances, and she has to speak the most elaborate verse—which I think only someone with a certain amount of experience can encompass.

'I think Juliet is to the young actress what Cleopatra is to the mature one. It is an enormous challenge and an enormous satisfaction and an enormous *joy*. We used to find when we played it in that last version at the New Theatre that it was a truly joyous performance. We were never got down by the tragedy because the youth and vitality of all those young people are so extreme and so marvellous that although tragedy hits them, catastrophe hits them, it does not destroy them because it is the tragedy of circumstance, of misfortune. It's just that things go wrong.

'I think that neither Romeo or Juliet are tragic characters in the classical sense in that tragedy is in their natures and therefore is inevitable for them. You feel that for them it shouldn't have been inevitable, they should have enjoyed their love more than Shakespeare allowed them to. They are the victims of hatred, malice and misunderstanding.'

Although both Romeo and Juliet take their own lives, there is no suggestion by Shakespeare that they have done anything wrong by so doing. But this is not the case with Ophelia. When Shakespeare was a boy of sixteen in 1579 a girl called Katherine Hamlet was found drowned in the Avon at Tiddington, just outside the town. It was necessary for a jury to be called to decide whether her death was the result of an accident or whether she had taken her own life. (This was still the form over two hundred years after Shakespeare wrote *Hamlet*, as we can read in contemporary newspaper accounts. If the verdict was suicide, then burial was at a crossroads with a stake driven through the heart of the corpse to prevent it wandering.)

It is too much of a coincidence to imagine that Shakespeare was not influenced by the death of Katherine Hamlet—and with such a name—when he wrote of the burial of Ophelia. 'Is she to be buried in Christian burial that wilfully seeks her own salvation?' asks the first gravedigger, and when her brother Laertes cries out against the lack of ceremony the priest says

> Her obsequies have been as far enlarg'd
> As we have warrantise: her death was doubtful

> And, but that great command o'ersways the order,
> She should in ground unsanctified have lodg'd
> Till the last trumpet; for charitable prayers,
> Shards, flints, and pebbles, should be thrown on her,
> Yet here she is allowed her virgin rites,
> Her maiden strewments, and the bringing home
> Of bell and burial.

Poor Katherine Hamlet. Poor Ophelia too; unlike most of the rest of Shakespeare's girls, she seems to have little or no will of her own—docile, frail, used by her father and the Court, she fragments into madness when faced with a frightening series of events.

Two views of Ophelia, one mid-nineteenth century, one modern, provide a fascinating contrast. Mrs Jameson says of her: 'Poor Ophelia. Far too soft, too good, too fair, to be cast among the briars of this working-day world and fall on the bleeding thorns of life ... she says very little and what she does say seems rather intended to hide than to reveal the emotions of her heart.'

She continues: 'While no one entertains a doubt of Ophelia's love for Hamlet it is a subject of dispute whether Hamlet loves Ophelia. Portia would have studied him, Juliet pitied him, Rosalind turned him over with a smile to the melancholy Jaques, Beatrice laugh at him outright, Isabel reason with him, Miranda wonder at him—but Ophelia loves him.'

Mrs Jameson saw Sarah Siddons play Ophelia, and it was something which made a deep impression on her. She quotes particularly:

Hamlet	I did love you once.
Ophelia	Indeed, my lord, you made me believe so.
Hamlet	You should not have believed me: for virtue cannot so inoculate our old stock but we shall relish it. I loved you not.
Ophelia	I was the more deceived.

'Those who have ever heard Mrs Siddons perform the play of *Hamlet* cannot forget the world of meaning, of love, of sorrow, of despair conveyed in those two simple phrases.

'Constance is frantic, Lear is mad, Ophelia is *insane*.' Even given the conventions of the time—and Mrs Jameson tended where possible to avoid mentioning or drawing attention to aspects of the plays she considered to be unpleasant—she has sympathy for the form Ophelia's madness takes, even when what the girl has to say is coarse and suggestive. 'It is right that in her madness she should exchange her bashful silence for empty babbling . . . say and sing precisely what she never would or could have uttered had she been in possession of her reason, it is so far from being an impropriety that it is an additional stroke of nature. I have myself known of one instance in the case of a young Quaker girl whose character resembled Ophelia and whose malady arose from a similar cause.'

Jan Kott, in *Shakespeare Our Contemporary*, says: 'Ophelia has been drawn into the big game. They listen in to her conversations, read her letters. It is true that she gives them up herself. She is at the same time part of the Mechanism and its victim. Politics hang here over every feeling and there is no getting away from it. All the characters are poisoned by it. . . .

'She knows that life is a hopeless business from the start. So she does not want to play her game with life at too high a stake. It is the events that compel her to overplay. Her boy-friend has been involved in high politics. She has slept with him. But she is a daughter of a Minister of the Crown; an obedient daughter. She agrees to her conversation being overheard by her father. Maybe she wants to save Hamlet. But she falls into the trap herself. The events have driven her into a blind alley from which there is no way out. An ordinary girl who loved her boy has been given by the scenario of history a tragic part.'

Whether or not Hamlet had actually seduced Ophelia before the play opens is a matter of debate. Some modern productions have suggested this was the case, but Robert Speaight—who has played in various productions over the years, and in the title role at the Old Vic in 1931—does not agree.

'I do not believe for a moment that Ophelia had been his mistress; her bawdy snatches in the mad scene might have come from the subconscious of a schoolgirl or a nun. To think otherwise is to confuse the parallelism of love and lust that runs through the play. Whatever Polonius and Laertes may have thought, Gertrude, over Ophelia's grave, admits that she had hoped "thou should'st have been my Hamlet's wife". That match was obviously not thought impossible and there is no reason to doubt Ophelia's assurance that Hamlet had "given countenance to his speech . . . with almost all the holy vows of heaven." . . . Ophelia was too weak to withstand the family pressures and she gave in.'

Ellen Terry said of Ophelia: 'The whole tragedy of her life is that she is afraid. I think I am right in saying that she is Shakespeare's only timid heroine. She is scared of Hamlet when trouble changes him from a *point device* lover, 'a glass of fashion' into a strange, moody creature. . . . She is scared of her father and dare not disobey him. She is scared of life itself when things go wrong. Her brain, her soul and her body are all pathetically weak.

'I think it should be suggested from the first that there is something queer about her which explains her wits going astray later on. Her father's murder is assigned as the reason, but it seems more likely that this shock developed an incipient insanity. Ophelia is really mad, not merely diplomatically mad, with grief. The mad were harshly treated in Shakespeare's day. Ophelia escaped the Dark House and whip but becomes avoided by everyone.'

Ophelia remains a knotty problem for an actress. Barbara Jefford says, 'You hardly see her after the beginning of the play. She has "O what a noble mind is here o'erthrown" and the next thing she's mad. You have this enormous time off stage and then you have to come on quite, quite mad. It's very difficult indeed. Did she and Hamlet have a real affair? There you are—you don't know. But in order to make Ophelia work you have to flesh it out and put things in which are not actually in the text in order to make it work for yourself as an actress.'

Suzanne Bertish, who played Ophelia to Derek Jacobi's Hamlet at the Old Vic in 1977, said she felt Ophelia to be a victim 'who gains her independence through madness. It's a tiny part, but absolutely crucial. A lot happens to Ophelia off stage which is unusual in Shakespeare—normally things happen on stage or you hear about them in a long speech, or a soliloquy or somehow, but Ophelia just rushes on and says "my lord, I've been so affrighted". The interesting scene has just happened off stage.'

She did not think Ophelia had the seeds of madness within her. 'I did not think that tendency to break down was there any more than it is in any of us. I think she was very deeply in love. We worked it out that she and Hamlet had had a very good relationship, which you didn't see, before the play started and suddenly that is destroyed, then her father disappears and they find his body. What has happened to him? She doesn't know. I felt that between the end of the play scene and when she reappears mad she had just rushed off and locked herself away and been in a room somewhere and people had forgotten her existence.'

Othello stands in the canon after *Hamlet* and immediately before *King Lear*. It was almost certainly written in 1604, and was certainly performed on 1 November of that year. As with *Measure for Measure*—written at about the same time—Shakespeare's source was Cinthio's *Hecatommithi*. In Cinthio's story a white girl marries a black man and runs away with him, and it is a cautionary tale designed to show that girls who behave in such a fashion and disobey their parents deserve to come to a bad end.

For many years Desdemona was considered a passive and gentle girl. The old view is summed up by Mrs Jameson, who says of her that 'gentleness gives the prevailing tone to the character, gentleness in its excess, gentleness verging on passiveness, gentleness which not only cannot resent but cannot resist'.

Yet there is nothing from Shakespeare's day down to our own which suggests total passivity in a girl who could defy her family to marry a man of another race. Coleridge gave the outraged conventional view when he said 'It would be something monstrous to conceive this beautiful Venetian girl falling in love with a veritable negro. It would argue a disproportionateness, a want of balance in Desdemona, which Shakespeare does not appear to have in the least contemplated.' Yet Shakespeare appears to have known very precisely what he was about.

As M. R. Ridley points out, Roderigo sees Desdemona's marriage as a "gross revolt", Brabantio sees in it a treason of the blood for which only her subjugation by charm can account, and for which she will incur a general mock; Nature, he says, could not err so preposterously "sans witchcraft".

Ridley says of Desdemona: 'She is often, perhaps usually, played as much less mature than I think Shakespeare intended her to be, as a sort of child-wife or second Ophelia. It is true that she has in her first pleading for Cassio, a child's innocent, though in the circumstances, fatal, persistence calculated to exasperate a much more slow-tempered man than Othello. In just this way a child tries to pin down a treat. . . . But there is much more to her than that. She has violated convention by her marriage, and knows it, she puts her case both to her father and the senate simply indeed, but with strong sense, courage, and plain speaking; she is a soldier's wife and fit to be so—even a man more besotted with love than Othello could not have addressed Ophelia as "My fair warrior"; she can stand up to Othello for the sake of what she thinks to be right, even when he is in a dangerous mood and few people would care to face him.'

He continues: 'There is one moment which always seems to me to put Desdemona's quality beyond doubt. After the brothel scene she is left "half asleep" and weeping, in the last extremity of bewildered distress. Yet, by Heaven knows what wrench of resolution, she pulls herself together for a formal banquet, at which she must entertain men who have seen her publicly struck, and, judging by the subsequent farewells, she acquits herself with at least decorum.'

Robert Speaight says the problem is to reconcile 'a maiden never bold' with the girl who prompted Othello's proposal, who did not shrink from a clandestine marriage, outrageous to society, and which broke her father's heart, and whose precocious strength of will is matched by a precocious capacity for submission. 'Her strength and her submission alike contribute to her undoing. Her importunate pleading for Cassio lends colour to the supposition of her guilt. Indeed her strength is at the root of her submissiveness, her innocence has a kind of obstinacy, which is not the obstinacy of Cordelia—for Cordelia stood up to Lear whereas Desdemona stands up to Othello for nothing except Cassio. With her last breath she denies Othello has killed her.

'Does the girl who challenged the mores of Venice with her marriage really believe that it is unthinkable for a woman to commit adultery or is she simply fencing with Emilia's worldly wisdom?' he asks. 'Why must she decide to renew her plea for Cassio at the very moment when Othello is enraged by the loss of the handkerchief? Why does she deny that it is lost? Why does she not say, quite simply, "I must have dropped it and I don't know where it is"? Desdemona's fate is intolerable; yet there is something in her almost masochistic submissiveness which irritates, very much as we are irritated by Othello's credulity.'

The matter of the handkerchief is what Barbara Jefford found the most difficult thing to accept. 'The hardest point for me in *Othello* was not to say "The handkerchief? I'll tell you" when he says, "Where is the handkerchief?" It is the crucial point of the play on which *everything* hinges. I felt that the person who Desdemona had been in the earlier part of the play would say, "Ah, wait a minute, Emilia was there when I lost it and she will know where it is—go to Emilia." Emilia by this time is shattered and she would say immediately that she gave it to her husband and the whole thing would collapse.

'These are the difficult and unreconciled problems you just have not to think about. She must have been a brave girl. She stood up to her father not only over a man they did not like but over a man of another race.'

Stratford's Desdemona in the 1979 season was Suzanne Bertish who played the part throughout as a very strong girl. She admits that she has a strong personality 'and I wasn't arbitrarily cast. There were certain lines I picked out in the text. They refer to her as our captain's captain, they say our general's wife is now the general. Then twice in the play she speaks like a lawyer. She says to Cassio "for thy solicitor would rather die" . . . where does she pluck this image from? Later she speaks of suborning witnesses, of an indictment. It's brilliant. Her father was a senator, there's no talk of her mother, and she must have listened to this kind of jargon since she was a child, it's part of her life.

'Oddly enough I thought of my own father when I came to play the part. He was a very strong man but also one of nature's innocents and he was optimistic almost until it made you want to scream. Desdemona has that quality. It's not weakness, it's very pure innocence. It is always believing the best of a situation which is what she does throughout.

'She is brave right from the beginning. Her father says, "Do you perceive in all this noble company, where most you owe obedience?" and she says in front of all those men that although hitherto she has shown a daughter's duty to a father she now has a husband and her duty is to him and then she goes on to say that she "saw Othello's visage in his mind". She's the only one in that scene who actually refers to him as being black—the others let it remain unspoken. Then, at the end of the play you still have to show that courage and I tried not to pre-empt that I knew Othello was going to kill me—how do you really *know* that someone is going to do that? *Othello* is a desperately human tragedy because jealousy is a monster born upon itself, begot upon itself. The point I most wanted to make about Desdemona was that goodness does not have to be weak.'

John Wain says of *Othello*: 'Othello and Desdemona can still fall in love. And when they do it, it is the differences between them, the uncharted gulf they have to cross in order to communicate, that brings them to destruction.'

The most usual date given for *King Lear* is 1606, and there is a fairly full report of a performance of it—in which Burbage played the name role—being given before the King at Whitehall on Boxing Day 1606. The most likely source—besides, of course, Holinshed's *Chronicle*—was an anonymous play, published in 1605, *The True Chronicle History of King Leir and his Three Daughters*, which although similar in some instances had a happy ending. No doubt Shakespeare drew too on old myths, and tales with similarities to *Lear* appear in a number of countries.

There is a Russian story of a king who asks his three daughters to say how much they need him. One says she needs him as much as silver, the second as much as gold, and the third as much as salt. This daughter is banished with a sack of salt round her neck until by magic the country loses all its salt. There is no way of preserving meat or fish and what food there is lacks all savour. The point having been made, salt and the third Princess are restored.

If *Macbeth* is classical tragedy, then *King Lear* is epic tragedy, taking place against a tremendous canvass on this 'great stage of fools'. Dr Johnson considered the end of *Lear* to be quite unbearable, and for many years Nahum Tate's version was the only one played. In this Cordelia, having been widowed, marries

Edgar and rules the kingdom happily ever after, while Lear is left to live out his days with them in peace.

Cordelia is a difficult role in that she says very little; what she feels is implied. Her first words reveal the girl. Both her sisters have given extravagant voice to their pretended feelings for their father. When he asks Cordelia what she can say to show even stronger feelings than her sisters, she replies 'Nothing, my lord.'

Lear	Nothing!
Cordelia	Nothing.
Lear	Nothing will come of nothing: speak again.
Cordelia	Unhappy that I am, I cannot heave
	My heart into my mouth . . .

There is a fascinating theory that in the original production of the play the same boy actor doubled the parts of the Fool and Cordelia. Technically it could be done, as Cordelia has left the stage before the Fool appears, and by the time she returns the Fool is on his way to Dover.

All we then learn of the Fool is from Lear when he says 'And my poor Fool is hanged.' Speaight says of Cordelia that 'the daughter becomes mother to the father. In her truth, which has a streak of her father's obstinacy, and in her tenderness, which has all his strength, she represents the bias of nature from which all her world has fallen, Edgar and Kent alone excepted. In a play devoted to the "marriage of true minds", she might well, as Nahum Tate proposed, have made a good wife for Edgar and 'her spirit lives on in him'.

Ellen Terry found Cordelia hard to play because she is 'so extremely reticent. She loves dearly, but never gushes'. She suggests that perhaps there are daughters who see the play and know exactly what Cordelia means when she says her love is richer than her tongue. She felt the crucial scene which points up Cordelia's nature is when she returns at the head of an army and finds Lear in a swoon, when she has not seen him since he banished her from his Court. 'Her love makes Lear's reconciliation with her easy. But she is shy and embarrassed when her father recovers consciousness. Still waters run deep in Cordelia.

'That sums up her character. Cordelia is a most difficult part. So little to say, so much to feel. Rarely does an actress fathom the depth of those still waters.'

One who seems to have done so is Peggy Ashcroft, for T. C. Worsley, writing in the *New Statesman* of the 1950 production of *Lear*—in which Sir John Gielgud played Lear and Peggy Ashcroft, Cordelia—said, 'She has more than any other actress the power of touching us simply by her posture and the atmosphere she distils.' Speaking of the reconciliation scene he says, 'The change from anxiety to flooding relief is beautifully done. Her "no cause, no cause" is marvellously dropped like two reassuring tears of forgiveness.'

Robert Speaight felt that 'when Lear entered with Cordelia dead in his arms, Shakespeare had reached the limit of a journey to the end of night which was also a journey to the edge of dawn. For this was not only a supreme *coup de théâtre*—the moment which has tempted all tragedians—but the fusion, perfectly articulated, of the cosmic and private agonies.'

The death of Cordelia takes our breath away because it has seemed right up to the end of the play that she is going to survive, and her hanging at the hands of Edmund is a terrible shock.

John Wain says that the savagery of Goneril and Regan was released by the folly of Lear and Gloucester. 'They are the instruments of nature's revenge for the disturbance of *pietas*—a revenge admittedly which steps beyond the bounds of the original offence and includes innocent beings in its wrath.' Cordelia's death is necessary, he says, because Lear then 'knows at last what love means.

'All this titanic expenditure of effort and suffering to teach two stupid old men how to love? Yes: and rightly; for the colossal extravagance of means, the cosmic excess of upheaval and waste, celebrates the range and importance of the nature of man.

> Upon such sacrifices, my Cordelia
> The Gods themselves throw incense!'

'Chimes at midnight'

Shakespeare wrote only one play in which all the female roles were set firmly in his own background—*The Merry Wives of Windsor*. In the rest such women appear as foils, companions, confidantes and maids to the daughters of dukes, kings and princes who take the leading roles. There are also a small number of country wenches who usually appear to hasten the plot or as contrasts to females of a different kind.

Women even outside the ranks of the aristocracy enjoyed more freedom and had a better life towards the end of the sixteenth century than they were to enjoy for a considerable time afterwards. The two waves of Puritanism, under Cromwell and then Victoria, were still to come, and they had not then had to sell themselves to the Industrial Revolution. The dragging of coal trucks on their hands and knees, the monstrous shifts at looms and in factories, were mercifully hidden in the future.

If we take as one source the *Case Book of Simon Forman*, the physician and astrologer who has left us among other things records of several of the first performances of Shakespeare's plays, then the wives of merchants, shopkeepers, vintners and craftsmen lived rich, full lives of their own. In A. L. Rowse's edited version of his papers, we see ladies of striking independence. Whether or not everything Dr Forman says is to be believed—he seems to have been something of an Elizabethan Frank Harris—such ladies spent much of their time not only consulting him about their medical problems but having their horoscopes cast to find out how their lovers regarded them, if their husbands would discover their

affairs; if, indeed, their husbands were likely to die. Liaisons
with such ladies—again if Forman is to be believed—were
easy to arrange. Here in the pages of his diary are the prototypes of
Mistress Page and Mistress Ford, making one wonder how those
two virtuous ladies might have reacted had Falstaff been more
attractive to them.

Also among his clients, sprinkled amid the great ladies, were the
young kept women, girls from poor backgrounds who were pretty
and intelligent and who had opted for a pleasant house and a good
income to be mistress to some middle-aged or elderly courtier.
Women came to find out if they were likely to become pregnant, if
they were pregnant. The desperate moral attitudes taken by the
Victorians were simply not known—when a young village girl
became pregnant it seems to have been treated more as a mishap or
a mistake, and if a marriage could not be arranged then neighbours
rallied round and did what they could.

Such a wench is Jacquenetta in *Love's Labour's Lost*. She has been
dispensing her favours to Costard the rustic clown and to Don
Armado, the proud Spanish aristocrat. She is the Dulcinea to his
Don Quixote.

She is also needed to play a part in the complicated business of
the letters, but we are told at the end of the play that she is, in
Costard's words, 'two months on her way'. How she fares we
never know, as her rural lover hands her over to her aristocratic
one, telling him that the child is his. Since he has sworn to devote
himself to good works for three years before taking up his
bargain—in line with the young lords whose fortunes we have
followed—the poor girl is likely to be in for a long wait.

Touchstone, the clown in *As You Like It*, is apparently more
prepared to stand by his girl, although his attitude to her is hardly
romantic. He agrees to see the priest with her, although he is
warned that his choice is not a very good one. 'This fellow will but
join you together as they join wainscot,' says Jaques. Touchstone
does not mind too much, telling the audience that if his marriage is
not a proper one then no matter, it is all the easier to leave his wife,
poor Audrey—a simpleton and a slut. When the Duke asks who
she is her swain replies, 'A poor virgin, sir, an ill-favoured thing,
sir, but mine own . . .'. 'Bear your body more seeming, Audrey.'

Since Audrey and Touchstone are there in part to show us one of the many facets of love with which the play deals (no doubt the most basic), Phebe and Corin show another face. Audrey herds goats, Phebe sheep, but here the resemblance ends. Audrey is content to be what she is, Phebe very definitely is not. She considers herself vastly superior to her peers and especially to her faithful lover, Corin. Later she gets her come-uppance when, like Olivia later, she falls in love with a girl disguised as a boy. The frozen virgin immediately unbends. 'Who ever lov'd that lov'd not at first sight?' she sighs. (This famous quotation is from Marlowe's *Hero and Leander*, published in 1598. *As You Like It* postdates its composition, then—but concerning the date of that composition there is no general agreement.) No matter how rude and cutting Rosalind is to Phebe, she positively dotes on her. Although she pairs off with Corin at the end, it seems unlikely that he will have a happy time of it.

In Maria in *Twelfth Night* we have a much more rounded character. She has been played in all kinds of ways—as a young, skittish girl, as a matronly housekeeper with a sense of humour, as a poor relation; all can be equally valid. By Elizabethan standards she must have considered herself to be rapidly passing marriageable age, but that could be at any time from eighteen years onward.

She can rail at Sir Toby Belch, while being devoted to him, and she is a regular confidante of her mistress, Olivia. Although she tries to hush up the festivities of Sir Toby and Sir Andrew Aguecheek, she finally joins in the singing and merriment with them because she obviously enjoys a good time. The untimely arrival of Malvolio in his nightshirt puts a damper on everything, and while he can shout at the two men it is not his place to send them away.

With Maria he can truly threaten. 'Mistress Mary, if you prized my lady's favour at anything more than contempt, you would not give means for this uncivil rule; she shall know of it, by this hand.'

From then on she hunts him down mercilessly. It is her original and inventive plan which is the comedy plot of the play. He will be tricked by her forgery of Olivia's handwriting into believing he has received a love letter from her. He is a prudish creature, 'a kind of Puritan', she says, contemptuously, a man without a sense of humour, and he will be made to laugh and smile like a loon. He is severe in his dress so she will make him get himself up in absurd yellow stockings and ribboned garters. He will be made the biggest fool in the world, and, even better, he may be taken as mad. The two scenes in which he first finds the letter and then acts on it are among the funniest Shakespeare ever wrote.

In his commentary on the play in 1968 Mahood says: 'Maria of course must be small and shrill and the sort of young woman who finds life intensely dramatic. But she is not a hoyden, and the part will probably be played as the kind of waiting-gentlewoman Shakespeare had in mind if the actress conceives of her as a poor relation with no dowry, anxious to find a husband before she is relegated to the shelf.'

There is a hard streak somewhere in Maria, too, for by the end of the play we feel sorry for Malvolio, full of self-love as he is. The rest of the conspirators are worried that they have actually gone too far by the time he has been confined to a dungeon and treated as a madman; Maria alone is unrepentant. Olivia puts pressure on Sir Toby to marry Maria as he had promised, half in jest, when she put the idea of the tricking of Malvolio up to him. But we feel no sense of the conventional happy ending the end of the play brings to the other pairs of lovers.

Emilia, in *Othello*, is married to the most unpleasant character Shakespeare ever created—Iago. Consumed with envy, totally without pity or warmth, she could have found nobody worse. When trying to find some reason to explain even to himself why he behaves as he does, he toys with the possibility that Emilia has been unfaithful to him with Othello but you cannot believe he takes it seriously.

Emilia goes along with him for two-thirds of the play, unaware of the havoc he is wreaking. She steals Desdemona's handkerchief, plays the part assigned to her, until she understands what is happening. Then she rounds first on Othello and it is she who stands up to him at the worst height of his jealous passion, when he makes his first attempt to murder Desdemona, and passionately defends her. Bravely, she later defies her husband to tell the truth about what has happened, knowing only too well what the result might be. He stabs her, and she dies.

It is in the scene between the two women, shortly before Desdemona's death, that Shakespeare contrasts most precisely the differences in values between the carefully nurtured, gentle girl from a wealthy and secure background and the earthy woman who has had to struggle for survival. Desdemona has finally admitted that Othello is jealous and, with some awful premonition of what is to come, sings the famous willow song. How can men be so terrible, she asks Emilia, how can they say such things, can there really be women who would 'abuse their husbands in this gross kind'?

Emilia	There be some such, no question.
Desdemona	Wouldst thou do such a deed for all the world?
Emilia	Why, would not you?
Desdemona	No, by this heavenly light!
Emilia	Nor I neither by this heavenly light; I might do't as well i' the dark.
Desdemona	Wouldst thou do such a deed for all the world?
Emilia	The world's a huge thing: it is a great price for a small vice.
Desdemona	In troth, I think thou wouldst not.
Emilia	In troth, I think I should; and undo't when I had done. Marry, I would not do such a thing for a joint-ring, nor for measures of lawn, nor for gowns, petticoats, nor caps nor any petty exhibition; but for the whole world—why, who would not make her husband a cuckold to make him a monarch? I should venture purgatory for't.
Desdemona	Beshrew me, if I would do such a wrong for the whole world.
Emilia	Why, the wrong is but a wrong i' the world; and having the world for your labour, 'tis a wrong in your own world, and you might quickly make it right.

Emilia is nothing if not a realist. She goes on to warn men in general to look to their wives, especially when they have affairs elsewhere. 'What is it that they do when they change us for others? Is it sport? I think it is: and doth affection breed it? I think it doth:

is't frailty that thus errs? It is so too. And have not we affections, desires for sport, and frailty as men have? Then let them use us well: else let them know the ills we do their ills instruct us to.' (This species of syllogistic protest is more than a little reminiscent of Shylock's great cry. Themes of reciprocity, equality of treatment and the inescapable relation between cause and effect Shakespeare has made his own.)

Dame Ellen Terry, who played the role, says of her: 'Emilia's life had made her cynical about virtue. No wonder! She would not be surprised at frailty even in Desdemona. And after all, is this frailty anything to make a fuss about? There is a curious anticipation of modern ideas in Emilia's attitude. . . . She has plenty of courage. She is alone with a murderer, a crazy murderer. She must know that she risks her life by arguing with him but she does not care. The slur on the dead woman makes her reckless. It is significant that the chivalrous champions of the honour of the living Hero, as of the dead Desdemona, should both be women.

'Significant and original, Shakespeare is one of the very few dramatists who seem to have observed that women have more moral courage than men.' Emilia is a gift for an actress and is one of those smaller roles Shakespeare wrote for both men and women, which must be a joy to play.

Like Emilia, Juliet's nurse has her feet firmly on the ground. She is perfectly prepared to help her darling meet Romeo, carry messages back and forth, connive at her marrying him. But when it all goes wrong and Romeo is banished, and there seems to be a chance to make good by a marriage between Juliet and the respectable Count Paris, then—why not? Nobody knew about the unofficial marriage and what they do not know need not hurt them.

The Nurse is prepared to stand up to old Capulet when he threatens her nursling as she refuses to countenance the marriage but when Juliet turns to her later, expecting not only comfort but total agreement with the course of action on which she is embarked, she has a shock. The Nurse replies:

> Faith, here 'tis: Romeo
> Is banished; and all the world to nothing

That he dares ne'er come back to challenge you;
Or, if he do, it needs must be by stealth.
Then, since the case so stands as now it doth,
I think it best you married with the county.
O, he's a lovely gentleman!
Romeo's a dishclout to him; an eagle, madam,
Hath not so green, so quick, so fair an eye
As Paris hath. Beshrew my very heart,
I think you are happy in this second match,
For it excels your first: or if it did not,
Your first is dead; or 'twere as good he were,
As living here, and you no use of him.

'Speakest thou from the *heart*?' inquires Juliet, and the Nurse replies that indeed she does, and 'from my soul too'. Juliet is appalled.

Although a number of well-known actresses have played the Nurse—Flora Robson is one that springs to mind, and Barbara Jefford played her in 1979 at the Old Vic—she is all too often played as if she were ninety. That could hardly have been the case if she were Juliet's wet-nurse and Juliet was barely fourteen. She was more likely to have been about fifty, although that probably seemed older then than it does now.

To understand her we do not even need to go back to Shakespeare's age: she comes down the centuries, the working-class or peasant woman from the country who has come in to work for the big family 'in service'. I admit to seeing her much like my late grandmother—full of practical common sense, loving and indulgent to her family but totally unable to understand the intense emotional and physical feelings of a sensitive adolescent. Marriage was a desirable end for many reasons—including financial ones, to provide a girl with a home and, of course, to have children—but romance did not enter into it.

Her humour is simple. The story of her late husband, 'a merry man', who when the toddling Juliet fell down said, 'Dost thou fall on thy face? Thou wilt fall backward when thou hast more wit' she repeats three times as the funniest of jokes. The Nurse is a necessary antidote to all the passion.

As we have seen from a look at the female roles in the Histories, women play only a relatively small role in *Henry IV* Parts 1 and 2 and in *Henry V*, except for the character of Mistress Quickly, hostess of the Boar's Head, Eastcheap. Hers is the famous inn where Falstaff, Prince Hal and their cronies meet, and it is she who looks after them, covers up for them, lends them money and generally cares for them in a way well in excess of that which duty demands. She appears only briefly in *Henry V*, where she tells of the death of Falstaff, and by the end of that play we are told in an aside that she is dead.

She was a character of whom Shakespeare was obviously fond, because as well as appearing in the *Henries* he used her again in *The Merry Wives of Windsor*, although she was translated from landlady to doctor's servant. One imagines she was too useful to let go as she could be brought into use in almost any situation. Perhaps anyway she was one of those creations who actually take on a life of their own as she managed, intrigued, passed on scandal and plunged into trouble up to her elbows.

The late Maureen Prior played the part in all three *Henry* plays and in the *Merry Wives* in Stratford and London during 1975/76, and she came to it with a certain amount of trepidation. She had not played a great deal of Shakespeare and admitted she had no particular reverence for him.

But she found the part took a hold on her in spite of herself. She discovered with some excitement a Warwickshire landlady whom she felt was just what Shakespeare had in mind—and she was convinced he did have somebody specific in mind to have written her the way he did. The lady she found, of uncertain years, was just as she had described when I was taken to see her.

This landlady was loud and knowledgeable. She had a habit of making strange noises over the bar like 'Whoops' and 'Ooch', and this same habit duly made its appearance on the stage of the Royal Shakespeare theatre. She would also lean confidentially across the bar, roll her eyes and in a penetrating whisper impart the latest piece of town scandal; and this too was duly noted.

Maureen Prior felt that Mistress Quickly was truly in love with Falstaff and fully aware that the class distinction between them, if nothing else, would prevent any true show of that affection. That was why she was endlessly prepared to let him sponge on her, borrow from her, never pay his bills and indeed treat her shamefully—she could not help herself. She also felt that Falstaff is almost always wrongly portrayed—as a fat, vulgar comedian and nothing more. He would, she felt, have been very much more than that—fat and red-faced maybe, but he would also have been very, very attractive, and it should be crystal-clear to the audience what all the characters in the play, and especially Prince Hal, find so attractive about such a hard-drinking, terrible rogue. In this she unconsciously echoed J. B. Priestley in an essay on the subject in his *Essays of Five Decades*.

It was the kind of part, she said, which should go to an actor with tremendous masculinity and charisma like Albert Finney, even if he did have to be padded out to play it. Then it would all make sense and especially Mistress Quickly's devotion to him.

She warmed to Shakespeare, she said, when a single phrase would float up and make the character clear, such as when Mistress Quickly is reeling off the virtues of various wines and comes to canaries: 'that's a marvellous searching wine—it perfumes the blood ere one can say, what's this?'

The second part of *Henry IV* is full of an autumnal quality. The King's life is drawing to an early close, the days of revelry are fast coming to an end—a sense of mortality is all around. It is even there in the most famous of the Boar's Head tavern scenes. Mistress Quickly may be no lady, but she knows, as they say, how to behave. Her friend Doll Tearsheet makes no such pretence, she is a hard-drinking, hard-swearing tart who responds to most verbal challenges with a round of abuse, but when Falstaff says, 'I am old', she says, 'and so I love thee better than I love e'er a scurvy young boy of them all.'

Women are remembered in another wonderful nostalgic scene, when the old justices Shallow and Silence reminisce with their cronies and Falstaff. Those were the great days when they were true 'Jack-the-lads': 'You had not four such swingebucklers in all the Inns of Court again.'

They chased the lights o' love, the 'bona robas', and old Shallow remembers Jane Nightwork and wonders if she is still alive. Falstaff says she is—but old. 'Nay, she must be old, she cannot choose but to be old; certain she's old; certain she's old and had Robin Nightwork, by old Nightwork, before I came to Clement's Inn.' 'That's fifty-five year ago,' mourns Silence. Ah, says Falstaff, in the line which sums it all up, 'We have heard the chimes at midnight.'

By the opening of *Henry V* Mistress Quickly has settled for marriage to one of Shakespeare's far less likeable rogues, the bragging Pistol. But it is she who nurses Falstaff on his death bed and it is she who in the second Act brings news of his death.

'He's in Arthur's bosom if ever man went to Arthur's bosom. 'A made a finer end, and went away an it had been any christom child; 'a parted even just between twelve and one, even at the turning o' the tide: for after I saw him fumble with the sheets, and play with flowers, and smile upon his finger ends, I knew there was but one way; for his nose was as sharp as a pen, and 'a babbled of green fields. How now, Sir John! quoth I: what, man! be of good cheer. So 'a cried out—God, God, God! three or four times. Now I, to comfort him, bid him 'a should not think of God; I hoped there was no need to trouble himself with any such thoughts yet. So 'a bade me lay more clothes on his feet: I put my hand into the bed and felt them, and they were as cold as any stone; then I felt to his knees, and so upward and upward, and all was as cold as any stone.'

It is said that Queen Elizabeth herself commissioned the *Merry Wives of Windsor* as she was so enchanted with Falstaff that she could not bear to see him killed off and begged for a further play, this one showing him in love. There is no hard proof of this, but almost certainly the play had its first performance before her in either 1600 or 1601. In this play Shakespeare ignores all that has gone before, this Sir John is younger, though no slimmer, and Mistress Quickly is the intriguing servant of the foppish French doctor. It is she who knits the strands of the plot together, informs the audience of what's toward and comes out well at the end, but she is not really the same person as she is in the other plays.

But it is the Merry Wives themselves, of course, who take the centre of the stage, and in their lives we have a clear picture of the lives of the women-folk of Shakespeare's friends and contemporaries in Stratford; indeed, of his own family. We see them running back and forth to each other's houses with messages and recipes, or simply to exchange gossip. Daughters' marriages are discussed and arranged (not always successfully), and husbands sent about their business. They are still attractive, and an element of spice is added to their lives if they embark on a harmless flirtation. They are well off enough to have servants, but not so rich that they cannot invite friends in to suppers which they have cooked themselves.

When Falstaff decides to pay court to both Mistress Ford and Mistress Page you can only feel sorry for the poor man for running his head into such a noose. There they are with some time on their hands, intelligent, probably a little bored, and ready for the fun they see they can have at his expense. By the time they have finished with him and he has been bundled into baskets of dirty linen, stumbled into ditches, disguised as an old woman and soundly beaten you feel he has been so tricked, cheated and swindled in his efforts to get them into bed with him that he can only have your sympathy.

Partly he is used by Mistress Ford to get her own back on her paranoidly jealous husband. The part of Ford with his desperate jealousy and mad disguises is a gem for an actor with a comic bent, and those who take it on usually play it to the hilt. Ben Kingsley at Stratford in 1979 looked like an Elizabethan Enoch Powell with small fanatical eyes and a toothbrush moustache, feverishly counting out his money to give to Falstaff, who is going to 'prove' Mistress Ford faithless. Ian Richardson in the 1975/76 Stratford production brought Ford to the edge of a rocketing hysteria, typified by his frantic search of his house for the fat knight. Not content with turning the whole place upside down, he was finally reduced to wrenching the lid off a tea caddy and peering inside it.

Ellen Terry said of *Merry Wives*: 'Here is the English race in a holiday mood enjoying itself very much as it does now on a Bank Holiday. I always see Mrs Ford as a rather demure little body, less free and easy in her manner than Mrs Page, yet with something in her eye which is distinctly coy—something which makes Ford's jealousy not altogether irrational. It is that something which accounts for her being rather flattered by Sir John's attentions. It is clear she is disappointed when she finds he is paying them to Mrs Page too.'

Merry Wives has been called a Shakespearean pot-boiler, but if it was, then it was a pot-boiler written with real love and feeling for the kind of people it portrays. It is a sunny, happy play, and you feel the women in it will continue to live happy, placid lives. No doubt having accustomed herself to her daughter's marriage to Fenton, Mrs Page will become a devoted grandmother, rushing over to tell her friend when her first grandchild cuts its first tooth.

No such secure happiness awaits the other earthy women. Emilia has died at the hands of her husband, Mistress Quickly of disease. Jacquennetta is left holding the baby, and Audrey will have Touchstone for just as long as he is prepared to stay with her. Juliet's Nurse has lost her child, and although Maria has achieved marriage with Sir Toby as she no doubt wishes, it hardly seems likely to promise great happiness. They have all heard the chimes at midnight, but now the revelry is done.

'Tigers, not daughters, what have you performed?'

Shakespeare wrote very little about truly evil women. Lady Macbeth is far too complex to be dismissed merely as the 'fiendlike Queen' and nothing more, and will have a chapter to herself. Other than Lady Macbeth there are the two wicked Queens, Tamora in *Titus Andronicus* and the lady merely described as 'Queen' in *Cymbeline*. The tigers of the title are the Misses Lear, Goneril and Regan as described by Albany. All four ladies are evil without any redeeming features unless you count the devotion of Cymbeline's queen to her lump of a son, Cloten.

The fifth lady dealt with in this chapter is not evil, but it seemed a suitable place to discuss her. Cressida is not evil, she is amoral, and Shakespeare wrote about her at a time when he seems to have been feeling deeply disgusted with women.

Tiger would be a kind description for Tamora, a Queen of Grand Guignol indeed. The whole of *Titus Andronicus* is one long, unadulterated horror story, nastier than anything even our current masters of the genre can dream up. It was an early play, published and produced in 1594, and A. L. Rowse feels that Shakespeare may have returned to Stratford two years earlier to write it, because all the theatres were closed that year owing to plague. There are doubts whether in fact Shakespeare was the author of all of it, but be that as it may it remains a nightmare tale still only rarely performed.

Briefly Lavinia, daughter of the general Titus Andronicus who is fighting against the Goths, is raped by the sons of Tamora, encouraged to do so by her. Although Tamora is a Gothic Queen (literally) she comes to be married to a decadent Roman Emperor, while at the same time having an affair with Aaron the Moor. In order to ensure Lavinia's silence, Tamora's lads cut off her hands and pull out her tongue.

In the course of the retribution for this ghastly event Tamora is served a pie by Titus at a dinner only to be told afterwards that it contains the flesh of her own children. Tamora remains throughout as evil, without showing any remorse. We do not know why she is as she is; there seems to be insufficient motivation for her actions.

A. L. Rowse is most perceptive about the horrors of *Titus*. He points out that the play was written when the rack and the Tyburn gibbet were still everyday features of life, and when the fires of Smithfield still burned in people's recent memories. So to a parallel with our own time. 'In the civilised Victorian age the play could not be performed because it could not be believed. Such is the horror of our own age, with the appalling barbarities of concentration camps and resistance movements paralleling the torture and mutilation and feeding on human flesh, of the play, that it has ceased to be improbable. We have the worst reasons for understanding how effective it was with the Elizabethans.' We can hardly point a finger at their taste when audiences nowadays have flocked to see the Edward Bond *Lear* or Peckinpah's slow-motion violence in the cinema.

Cymbeline's Queen is nothing like so dreadful. She is more like the traditional wicked stepmother of fairy tales, such as the wicked Queen in *Snow White*. In fact, her treatment of Cymbeline's daughter Imogen has parallels with that fairy story. Jealous of Imogen's youth, goodness and beauty, she is prepared to put up with her so long as she imagines she will marry her oafish son, Cloten, and so make him heir to the throne—for the plot depends on the assumption that Imogen's brothers are dead.

When Imogen not only refuses but marries the man of her choice the Queen first turns Cymbeline against her, then tries to poison her and finally bribes a servant to take her away and kill her. Instead he tells Imogen what has happened, and helps her to escape. The Queen then drops out of the story, having played her part in the plot, and when we hear of her again she has just died.

Whether her death was self-inflicted we are not told. When asked by Cymbeline 'How ended she?' the doctor replies

> With horror, madly dying, like her life;
> Which, being cruel to the world, concluded
> Most cruel to herself.

She has never seemed real, and must be an unrewarding part for an actress. An attempt to jazz her up in the 1974 Stratford version resulted in her wearing an extraordinary wig so long that it was still coming on stage one side as she exited off the other. Apart from raising a few smiles it still did not bring the character to life.

We never see Goneril or Regan either in anything but an unsavoury light. When we first meet them they are totally hypocritical, telling their old father what he wants to hear. Who loves me most? he demands, and naturally Goneril and Regan vie with each other.

> I love you more than words can wield the matter;
> Dearer than eyesight, space and liberty,

says Goneril. Regan tries to cap that, her sister comes too short, she says, her father's love is everything in the world to her, nothing else matters. It is left to the honest Cordelia to say that she has nothing to add. She loves her father as she should, no more, no less; and from there stems the action which is to lead to tragedy for everybody.

Goneril and Regan have no saving graces. The animal metaphor is used more than once; not only do they appear like tigers but they are also described as wolves. We watch them first turn on their father once they have got all they want, then revolt against him. Both lust after the bastard, Edmund. It is Regan who helps to put out Gloucester's eyes and at the end of the play she is poisoned by Goneril, who then kills herself.

Judi Dench found real problems playing Regan. 'It was actually a part I had always wanted to play, in fact I wanted to play it passionately. I thought it was wrong that in the first scene in come Cinderella and the Ugly Sisters. I thought I'm tired of that, I'm tired of seeing just two snarling girls. I didn't want to make them sympathetic, I didn't want to try and make them good characters because they are rank bad ones but they're so two-dimensional. They come in evil and go on being evil and that's Regan. She has one wonderful line:

> In my true heart
> I find she names my very deed of love;
> Only she comes too short.

'As soon as she says it Cordelia more or less says you snake, you don't mean it—straight away! You're not given a chance, it's like Rosencrantz and Guildenstern. So I thought perhaps I should show extreme nervousness with Lear, because where's the mother? I was obsessed with this and was sent up rotten about it. But I was determined to find something in that girl which maybe gave a clue as to why she behaved as she did. So when she spoke to Lear every time, I stammered a little, not with anybody else but with him. I appeared extremely nervous. But I was a tyrant when he wasn't there—there was too much of her father in her in a way.

'Well, of course, it still didn't work and I was absolutely awful.' The production was updated almost to today and she found this no help either. 'The costumes didn't help. We all came on in white dresses with blue orders of the Garter across us and tiaras and so on. They were wonderful costumes in themselves, but I couldn't reconcile what Regan wore with the sort of person who would then go on to put out somebody's eyes. She would have shot him or injected him or something, but Lear's was a barbaric era. I couldn't reconcile myself to the updating, the events of the play are too primitive, too stark. I felt beaten.

'In the end an awful kind of hysteria took over and John Woodvine and I couldn't meet each other's eyes. He used to bring on an eye in a plastic bag, then palm it, and at some stage during the scene with Gloucester he would fling it against the wall. That was all right until the night when I came in and saw they hadn't removed the eye from the previous evening—and I was away. The whole thing was terrible—*I* thought.

'I finally gave up the part after a friend had come to see me in it. I had to wear a long grey fur coat and a kind of peaked fur hat and he said for God's sake don't run across the stage dressed like that, somebody will shoot you. . . . That was the end.'

Perhaps critic John Barber should have the last word on Goneril and Regan. Pale and murderous, he says, it is difficult to understand 'the sub human indecency' Shakespeare wrote into these women.

Troilus and Cressida was acted in 1602, and Shakespeare drew on two sources for it. In 1598 Chapman had published his first translation of the *Iliad*, while obviously Shakespeare had long known Chaucer's *Troilus and Criseyde*. He drew characters from both sources, but being Shakespeare made some his own. Although Ulysses and Thersites both appear in the *Iliad*, it is Shakespeare who makes them the realistic and ironic commentators on the action of the play.

As A. L. Rowse points out, it has never been a particularly popular play. He puts this down to its nature being 'caviare to the general, who do not much care for satire, especially on themes so dear to its great good heart—love and war'. It is a play for intellectuals, he says, and was probably written for a private performance, possibly at the Inns of Court since there is much legal word play in it. Its message, he says, is clearly 'a plague on both your houses'.

The play seems to have been written, too, following a period of bitterness and disillusion suffered by its author, and there are obvious suggestions that his betrayal by the Dark Lady of the Sonnets was reflected in the character of Cressida. She is not, I think, a character that appeals much to women, but not surprisingly she continues to intrigue men. There is, however, a touch of Emilia's realism about her.

In Chaucer's original she was a young widow, but Shakespeare makes her an unmarried girl. However, she is obviously no novice in the ways of men and that knowledge includes the likely gains to be made by withholding or granting sexual favours.

> Yet I hold off. Women are angels, wooing;
> Things won are done; joy's soul lies in the doing
> That she beloved knows nought that knows not this.
> Men prize the thing ungain'd more than it is.

After spending the night with Troilus, she says:

Prithee, tarry:
You men will never tarry.
O foolish Cressid! I might have still held off,
And then you would have tarried.

To Jan Kott, for all its cynicism, *Troilus and Cressida* remains a
grim play. 'Menelaus is a cuckold, Helen is a tart, Achilles and
Ajax are buffoons. But the war is not buffoonery. Trojans and
Greeks die in it, Troy will perish in it.'

He finds Cressida totally intriguing. 'Cressida is one of the most
amazing Shakespearean characters, perhaps just as amazing as
Hamlet. And, like Hamlet, she has many aspects and cannot be
defined by a single formula.

'This girl could have been eight, ten or twelve years old when
the war started. Maybe that is why war seems so normal and
ordinary to her that she almost doesn't notice it and never talks
about it. Cressida has not yet been touched, but she knows all
about love, about sleeping with men; or at any rate she thinks she
knows. She is inwardly free, conscious and daring. She belongs to
the Renaissance but she is also a Stendhal type akin to Lamiel, and
she is a teenage girl of the mid-twentieth century. She is cynical or
rather would-be cynical. She has seen too much. She is bitter and
ironic. She is passionate, afraid of her passion and ashamed to admit
it. She is even more afraid of feelings. She distrusts herself. She is
our contemporary because of this self-distrust, reserve and need
of self analysis. She defends herself by irony . . . there is no place
for love in this world.'

When she goes over to the Greeks 'she has realized that beauty
arouses desire. She can still mock. But she already knows she
will become a tart. Only before that happens she has to destroy
everything so that not even memory remains.'

Actor Robert Speaight thinks that Cressida was probably as truly
in love with Troilus as her nature allowed her to be—but she
realizes her own frailty. 'Cressida, like Helen, is a daughter of the
game.' Cressida's saving grace is to have no illusions about herself.

There are analogies between Hamlet's disillusionment with
Gertrude and that of Troilus with Cressida. 'But there is more
stuff in Cressida than in Gertrude, and more subtlety in
Shakespeare's portrait of her. Weak as she may be, she has none of

Gertrude's lymphatic passivity; to put it bluntly she would have been more fun to seduce. And even when she has gone her way with Diomed, she can still write to Troilus. What did she say? We do not know because he does not read the letter. This is one of the several unanswered questions in what have been called the "problem plays".'

'The fiendlike queen'

Dr Johnson dismisses Lady Macbeth briefly: 'Lady Macbeth is merely detested', he says, and goes on to other matters. Yet she has continued to intrigue and puzzle most commentators, critics and actresses over the centuries.

The source for *Macbeth* again seems to have been Holinshed, who wrote at some length about him. His account begins long before the events commencing Shakespeare's play, but the broad outline is all there, from Macbeth's meeting with some 'goddesses of destinie or else some nymphs or feiries', who prophesy he will become King, to his death at the hands of a man not born of woman when Birnam Wood has come to Dunsinane. Banquo, Macduff and the murder of Lady Macduff and her children are also there, but Lady Macbeth makes only one appearance, and that is as the urger and possibly the instigator of Duncan's murder.

The historical Macbeth reigned in Scotland from 1039 to 1056 A.D., and little is known about him, although it would appear that one of the reasons for Lady Macbeth's desire to kill Duncan was that of family revenge—her grandfather Kenneth of Scotland had been killed by Duncan's father, Malcolm II, and the blood feud had continued down the generations.

The play was first published in the Folio of 1623, and its first recorded performance was in the spring of 1611. Witchcraft was very much in the air; James I had himself written a treatise on the subject, in which he had a deep and overwhelming belief. Treason too was topical in the aftermath of the Gunpowder Plot. A play which combined a Scottish king, treason and witchcraft all in one plot had obvious appeal.

The first commentary on an actual production is by Dr Simon Forman in *The Book of Plays*. He trundles briskly through the plot, says that Macbeth 'thorowe the persuasion of his wife did that night Murder the kinge in his own Castell' and continues, 'obserue Also how machbets quen did Rise in the night in her Slepe & walke and talked and confessed alle, & the doctor noted her wordes.'

The play then had an extremely chequered career, being presented only rarely in the early years, and from 1674 to 1744 was performed only in an adapted version by D'Avenant. We know the names of those who played Macbeth, from the first one— Burbage—through Garrick to the Gielguds, Oliviers and McKellans of recent times, but of the early Lady Macbeths there is little record. She was a subsidiary character to many of the great actor-managers.

It has become known as the play above all others which is dogged by ill luck. Quoting from it at any time is bad luck in a theatre: in rehearsal it must never be named, but referred to only as the Scottish play. Stories abound of disaster striking those taking part, or technical faults which arise inexplicably, of unhappy casts.

Producers and directors have been divided over the years as to the emphasis given to the place of witchcraft in the story and how deeply involved Lady Macbeth was in this aspect. Trevor Nunn in his 1974 version went overboard for witchcraft almost to the exclusion of everything else, and also went in for a highly elaborate production. Two years later he attempted it again and this time produced what must be one of the finest productions it has ever received—pared down to the minimum, played in the round in a studio and without an interval.

Before we come to the actresses who have played the part discussing it in their own words—and we are fortunate that both Sarah Siddons and Dame Ellen Terry were so obsessed with the role that they left detailed notes behind on how they saw it—it is worth while to look at how some commentators have viewed it, and how critics have reacted to it in performance. Men have tended to look more for Macduff's 'fiendlike Queen', while women see her more in the round.

A. L. Rowse expresses the dilemma of just what she is: 'Is Lady Macbeth possessed when she calls on the powers of evil to unsex her, fill her full of cruelty and expel from her all signs of grace? Jacobean spectators would take this, like the Queen in *Hamlet*, literally. Shakespeare leaves the question open. We are at liberty to interpret as we will, but there is no doubt about the fact of evil, the existence of the phenomenon. In our time we have seen Macbeth's fearful nightmare re-enacted in the highest place on the public scene. Rule by murder gives no security.'

Hazlitt said: 'She is a great, bad woman who we hate, but whom we fear more than we hate. Her fault seems to have been an excess of that strong principle of self interest and family aggrandisement not amenable to the common feelings of compassion, failure and justice, which is so marked a feature in barbarous nations and times.'

Coleridge says: 'Her constant effort throughout the play was to bully conscience. She was a woman of a visionary and a daydreaming turn of mind, her eye fixed on the shadows of her solitary ambition; and her feelings abstracted, through the deep musings of her absorbing passion, from the common life sympathies of flesh and blood. But her conscience, so far from being seared, was continually smarting within her; and she endeavoured to stifle its voice and keep down its struggles.'

W. Moelwyn-Merchant, commenting on the role, says: 'Lady Macbeth's willed submission to demonic powers, her unequivocal resolve to lay her being open to the invasion of witchcraft, is held in dramatic contrast to the painful, casuistic deliberations of Macbeth. She takes her appropriate dramatic place in the company of those whose supernatural status is obscure. Are the weird sisters witches, norns, fates or hallucinations?'

In 1963 Professor L. C. Knights, in an essay entitled 'How many children has Lady Macbeth?' took to task all those—and especially the critic A. C. Bradley—who seek for reality in Shakespeare's characters, seeing it as unnecessary, since the plays are poems, pure and simple. Bradley had indeed seen Lady Macbeth as a real woman, rushing to disaster in the dark and so needing 'a light by her continually'. It is untrue to Shakespeare, he says, to see Macbeth merely as a hard-hearted, cowardly criminal and Lady Macbeth as a whole-hearted fiend. 'They are two characters fired

by the same passion of ambition and to a considerable extent are
alike. . . . They support and love one another. They suffer together
and if, as time goes on, they drift a little apart, they are not vulgar
souls to be alienated and recriminate when they experience the
fruitlessness of their ambition, they remain to the end tragic, even
grand.'

Lady Macbeth goes forward on 'sheer force of will, she leans on
nothing but herself. Her greatness lies almost wholly in courage
and force of will—not intellect. The witches are nothing to her.'
When we see her later as Queen, he says, the glory has already
faded and she is disillusioned and weary from lack of sleep.
'Henceforth she has no initiative, the stem of her being has been
cut through. She sinks slowly down through the disorders of sleep
to madness. Much that is good, much that is piteous is there. By her
lights she has been a perfect wife. She gave her husband the best
she has.' The fact that she does not return the terms of affection he
uses to her is no indication of want of love. 'She urges, appeals,
reproaches for a practical end but she never recriminates.'

Prints of mid-eighteenth-century productions show a Mrs Yates
in a huge hooped skirt, clutching two daggers, David Garrick and
Mrs Pritchard in the roles looking as if they had just left a
contemporary soirée. A critic of Garrick's production says:
'Players have long since removed Lady M from this scene (the
Banquet). A London audience we may suppose not to be so critical
as that of Athens, or Oxford or Cambridge could supply. Many
years since I have been informed an experiment was hazarded
where the spectators would see Lady Macbeth's surprise and
fainting but however characteristic such behaviour might be, it
was not thought proper to venture on the lady's appearance any
more. Mr Garrick thought that even so favourite an actress as Mrs
Pritchard would not, in the situation, escape derision from the
gentlemen in the upper regions.'

Coming nearer our own time, few Lady Macbeths seem to have
suited the critics. Sybil Thorndike's performance in the 1916
Macbeth, directed by Ben Greet and with Robert Atkins as
Macbeth, moved an unnamed critic on *The Stratford Herald* to say:
'Sybil Thorndike as Lady Macbeth was being pushed by the
character instead of dominating it with what resources she

possesses. She has not that sweep and all-encompassment of personality to achieve the part effectively. Sybil Thorndike was wearing gloves much too big for her and was too prone at times to reduce the woman to the standard of the "little cat". She had too much weight which was not exactly heavy.'

In 1947 Diana Wynyard played the role at Stratford with Godfrey Tearle as Macbeth, directed by Anthony Quayle. Her performance prompted Harold Hobson to say: 'For some reasons hidden to me she has been dressed in a rag bag of garishly coloured garments which, till she speaks, makes her resemble a palmist on a seaside pier.' Another critic said instead of playing a great bad woman, she played it as 'A gentle sweet one doing her best to be bad with the aid of a chalk white face, a dark wig and draperies suggesting something between a squaw and Miss Gingold's more extravagant music lectures.'

The 1951 Gielgud production with Margaret Leighton as Lady Macbeth pleased Elizabeth Frank of the *News Chronicle* but disappointed H. Conway of the *Standard* who anyway felt Siobhan McKenna had stolen the show as Lady Macduff.

In 1955 the Oliviers essayed it, and nobody liked Vivien Leigh. Patrick Gibbs of the *Daily Telegraph* said she was hard and cold and that 'physical attraction is no help in this part'. Fergus Cashin of the *Mirror* went further. 'Vivien Leigh has never looked more beautiful and striking than she did last night as Lady Macbeth . . . her hair was flaming red, she wore large, pendant earrings and a clinging gown of shining green. But she spoke her terrible, haunting lines like a run-down gramophone record in a bucket.'

Trevor Nunn's 1976 production met with an unenthusiastic response, B.A. Young of *The Financial Times* saying that in the sixth round of the contest between Shakespeare and the RSC, Shakespeare had lost again. Nicol Williamson was the Macbeth, with Helen Mirren as Lady Macbeth, following in a recent tradition of the role going to pretty, young and sexy ladies. She completely overthrew Harold Hobson, however, who had a penchant for blonde sex-kittens.

He positively rhapsodized: 'An increase to our delight is the civilised, controlled, intelligent and irresistable sexuality of Helen Mirren's Lady Macbeth. It would be mere male chauvinism to deny that Miss Mirren plays everyone else off the stage. When the stage was occupied only by Macbeth himself, Macduff and so on, I was wishing the author would get rid of them and let us see what was happening to this marvellous actress. I really do regret that Shakespeare never knew Miss Mirren. We would then have had a different play.' This gave me pause for thought, particularly as I remember a gentleman well up in the hierarchy of *The Sunday Times* who had told me he would never employ a female theatre critic because she might fancy the actors.

Leaving the reviewers behind on that bizarre thought, we come to three actresses, each divided by the span of a century, who have been regarded as among the greatest interpreters of the role—Mrs Siddons, who played it in the eighteenth and early part of the nineteenth centuries, Dame Ellen Terry who played it a hundred years later and Judi Dench, the Lady Macbeth of the Royal Shakespeare Company's 1976 production, with a performance which cleared the board of acting awards.

Sarah Siddons wrote about the role at length, taking it scene by scene and also as a whole. She said: 'In this astonishing creature one sees a woman in whose bosom the passion of ambition has obliterated all the characteristics of human nature; in whose composition are associated all the subjugating powers of intellect and all the charms and grace of personal beauty.' She sees Lady Macbeth as 'a character which I believe is generally allowed to be most captivating to the other sex—fair, feminine, nay, perhaps even fragile. Such a combination only, respectable in energy and strength of mind and captivating feminine loveliness, could have composed a charm of such potency as to fascinate a hero so dauntless, a character so aimiable, so honourable as Macbeth, to seduce him to brave all the dangers of the present and all the terrors of the future world.'

Writing of the murder scene, she said: 'By her opprobious aspersion of cowardice, she chases the gathering drops of humanity from his eye and drives before her impetuous and destructive career all those kindly charities, those impressions of loyalty, pity and gratitude, which, but the moment before, had taken possession of his mind.' By Act III 'the worm that never dies gnaws her heart. She is no longer as she was, behold the striking

indications of sensibility, nay, tenderness and sympathy'. By Act
V, 'behold her now with wasted form, with wan and haggard
countenance, her starry eyes glassed with the ever-burning fever
of remorse and on their lids the shadow of death—awake or asleep,
the smell of innocent blood incessantly haunts her imagination.'

That the role truly haunted her is shown in her description of
how she approached it. 'It was my custom to study my characters
at night when all the domestic cares and business of the day was
over. On the night preceding that in which I was to appear in this
part for the first time, I shut myself up as usual and commenced my
study of Lady Macbeth. As the character is very short I thought I
should soon accomplish it. Being then only 20 years of age, I
believed that little more was necessary than to get the words into
my head, for the necessity of discrimination and the development
of character had at that time of my life scarcely entered my
imagination. I went on with tolerable composure in the silence of
the night (a night I can never forget) until I came to the
assassination scene when the horrors of the scene rose to such a
degree that it made it impossible for me to go further. I snatched
up my candle and hurried out of the room in a paroxysm of terror.'
She rushed up the stairs, she says, terrified by their creaking and
convinced that the rustle of her silk dress was the sound of an
oncoming shroud and finally fell asleep, fully dressed, on top of her
bed with her candle still burning in its holder. Lady Macbeth, she
says, 'having impiously delivered herself up to the excitements of
hell is abandoned to the guidance of the demons she has invoked.'

Dame Ellen Terry was fascinated with how Siddons portrayed
the role, saying that according to accounts of her contemporaries,
she played it like a tigress, 'an exultant savage', exiting from the
sleepwalking scene like a whirlwind, yet it would seem that
Siddons herself 'did not see the role like that'. Dame Ellen gave her
views in a lecture, later published in 1932. She goes on to say that
she had been told a story about the Siddons Lady Macbeth by Sir
Henry Irving.

An old family friend, Mr A, had met John Philip Kemble in a
coffee-house. This Mr A had tried to approach Kemble, but had
been told by the proprietor that he was a man who easily lost his
temper, and was also very deaf. However, nothing daunted, Mr A

approached him and asked how Siddons portrayed the sleep-walking scene. An almost Pinteresque exchange then took place, with the deaf Kemble mishearing every question. Finally, 'What was her method in the scene?' Mr A bellowed. 'Method? Sarah's method? Let me see—*She never moved.*' 'I don't know', continues Ellen Terry, 'what Mr A made of this but it conveys a great deal to me about Mrs Siddons' treatment of the scene. Her whirlwind exit must have been tremendous after such immobility.'

Dame Ellen was indeed a famous Lady Macbeth, a role of which she says: 'It seems strange to me that anyone can think of Lady Macbeth as a sort of monster, abnormally hard, abnormally cruel or visualize her as a woman of powerful physique with the muscles of a prize fighter. But it is clear from the records of some performances of the part and from portraits of actresses who gave them, that it can be done. I conceive Lady Macbeth as a small, slight woman of acute nervous sensibility and now I must tell you why. I don't think my conception is contradicted by the lines in which Lady Macbeth reproaches Macbeth for his pusillanimity. As I construe them they support it.

> I have given suck, and know
> How tender 'tis to love the babe that milks me:
> I would, while it was smiling in my face,
> Have pluck'd my nipple from his boneless gums,
> And dash'd the brains out, had I so sworn
> As you have done to this.

'Are not the lines capable of this construction "I would do all that I couldn't do, all that would be utterly false to every natural instinct and feeling of mine, rather than break such an oath as the one you have sworn". This frenzied appeal is surely the expression of the desperation Lady Macbeth feels at the sudden paralysis of Macbeth's faculties in the hour of action. He must be roused, he *must* be roused. Is all they have gone through to be for nothing? She is beside herself. We really ought not to take her wild words as a proof of abnormal ferocity.

'She has never failed her husband yet. The relation between them is not that of master and subject. They are on the terms of equals. She has always been fully cognizant of his plans and helped

to carry them out. Macbeth calls her "my dearest partner in
greatness" and it is as partners they engage in crime. The wife is
compelled to take up the burden of the action when the husband,
who being a dreamer finds it intolerably heavy, lays it down. Lady
Macbeth's nervous force sustains her until Duncan's murder is
accomplished. Then she collapses and faints. I suppose we can say
that's womanly!

'Henceforth she is troubled with thick coming fancies. In plain
prose she has a nervous breakdown. She is haunted by the horror of
the murder. It preys on her mind and saps her physical strength.
She dies of remorse. Surely this is good evidence that she is not the
tigress type, mentally or physically.'

Judi Dench played the part during a season when she was also
playing Beatrice, Adriana (the shrew in *Comedy of Errors*) and
Regan, in the main auditorium at Stratford with *Macbeth*, in the
round, at the Other Place. It later transferred to London. She had
worried when Trevor Nunn first offered her the role that she
would not feel equipped to play it although she had played it before,
in 1963. This production was directed by Frank Hauser and starred
John Neville and it toured West Africa. 'They found it terribly
funny—I honestly don't know why. It was most disconcerting to
be greeted with such hilarity every night—lines like "the thane of
Fife had a wife" were greeted with gales of mirth, they nearly fell
off their seats. They were only quiet during the witchcraft bits.

'Yet when I came to study the play again for Trevor I found that
I had absorbed a great deal from the text although his production
was nothing like that of Hauser's. It still worried me though and
I've always been obsessed somewhat by the view of Edith Evans
that there is a missing scene in the play, between the Macbeths
before the sleepwalking scene—which is why she would never
play the part. But when I came to work on it again I found I no
longer believed this.'

She feels that Lady Macbeth is a mature woman. 'If you play it
as a young, pretty girl then it is the sexuality of Lady Macbeth
which drives Macbeth but I don't think it can be entirely that.
think there is a tremendous passion between them, a truly animal
passion, but I don't think it is that that drives him on—otherwise it
makes him a very weak man indeed.

Ophelia: Mrs Patrick Campbell (1897)

Above. Lady Macbeth: Mrs Yates (1768)

Above right. Lady Macbeth: Mrs Siddons (1812 print)

Above far right. Lady Macbeth: Ellen Terry (1888)

Right: Lady Macbeth: Judi Dench (1976)

Above far left. Juliet: Fanny Kemble (1829)

Above left. Juliet: Ellen Terry (1882)

Left. Juliet: Peggy Ashcroft (1935)

Above. Cleopatra: Miss Younge (1772)

Above left. Cleopatra: Miss Glyn (1849)

Above right. Cleopatra: Ludmilla Storozheva (1962)

Left. Cleopatra: Lillie Langtry (1890)

Right. Cleopatra: Janet Suzman (1972)

Cleopatra: Glenda Jackson (1979)

'I believe that Lady Macbeth is driven on by the most tremendous ambition, *not* for herself but for her husband. And that is why it is essential to make those two people recognizable. They must be two people that we can recognize immediately, and they must not come in merely as the wicked King and Queen.

'It is essential too that he should also be seen to have that streak of ambition. When the witches say their piece, Macbeth is not *really* surprised—you feel he has already thought of it and may well have discussed it with Lady Macbeth earlier. When he does tell her what is in his mind, she feels that this is the one thing the man she adores really wants and must have. I don't think she cares about being Queen but she's obsessed about him being King. Therefore I believe the conjuring up of the spirits is not something she does. It's something she knows about like women at fairs or conjuring up the devil, something one could do by a Black Mass depending on whether or not one wants to do that kind of thing. It is certainly something she would know about, but I feel that what she has is something more to do with that farsightedness they still have in Scotland.

'When it came to the conjuring up of the spirits, I made it that she maybe wanted to pull back, maybe she felt it had all gone too far. I think the apex of the play for her is after the coronation and she thinks "that's it, we're here". Then comes the first moment when she feels she is rejected and finds it impossible to understand—this was something we worked out very carefully between us.

'Because of that production in the round, it was a great help to sit through the plotting of the other murders as if she was just outside the door. It is after this she walks in and he walks out and never looks back at her and after that the rift just gets larger. The hairline crack widens as she is more and more excluded. He wants to go on and she wants to withdraw.

'I don't think she knew about the other murders. She certainly didn't know about the proposed murder of Banquo. The next time you see them they are both troubled by dreams and she says what's the matter, come to bed, what kind of life is this? She's become excluded not only from his life, his bed and his social presence but from his plans and that has never happened before.

'Then comes the Banquet and she fully realizes that he's
beginning to crack up and she tries desperately to pull him back
from the edge. By the end of the Banquet she is absolutely
exhausted and it must be seen as a natural progression of events
which is to come. She's wracked by dreams. There's all the
speculation as to how did she die but I don't think it matters. You
must feel by the time of the sleepwalking scene that here is a
woman on the very edge of madness. I think the cry she makes
should be like a death rattle, after which she simply ceases to exist.
She's so wracked by guilt over the murder and it has all gone
wrong, this action which was supposed to bring about the answer
to all her dreams.

'One of the reasons why it worked so well was the style of
production. Someone asked why wasn't there an interval and it
was because the audience shouldn't be let off the hook, just as they
are not let off the hook. There was something about doing it in that
form which made the action inevitable. Once they had stepped
into that circle there was no going back.

'As a girl I was taken to see a bullfight in Spain. I was appalled
and had to be taken out as I was absolutely hysterical. The sight of
that black bull coming in and knowing that by fair means or
foul—and some of the means were certainly foul—that the bull
was going to be dead at the end appalled me. It wasn't ever going
to be fair. It was the inevitability of death that was so chilling and
that is right there in *Macbeth*. We kept saying at rehearsals do let's
tell the story, there may be children coming who don't know it or
how it ends, but truly, once the third witch has said "All hail,
Macbeth! that shalt be King hereafter", and Macbeth has gone on
to do the murder then they are both on the wheel and they cannot
possibly get off.'

'A lass unparallel'd'

Few characters in any play of any age have such a build-up as Cleopatra. Says Enobarbus,

> Age cannot wither her, nor custom stale
> Her infinite variety; other women cloy.

She is all things to all men, and she is likely to be the greatest challenge any actress will attempt in a lifetime. Possibly because of the difficulties of casting the protagonists, *Antony and Cleopatra* has been performed comparatively rarely.

Chaucer was one of the first major writers to touch on the legend, and shortly before Shakespeare wrote his play there were a number of others on the same theme—in French, Italian and English. Most popular was the *Tragedie of Antony* published in 1595 from a translation of *Marc Antoine* by Robert Garnier which had been written in 1578.

Antony and Cleopatra may have been written in 1606 almost immediately after *Macbeth*. For his source Shakespeare went to Plutarch, as he did for *Coriolanus* and *Julius Caesar*. Plutarch took a highly critical view of Cleopatra, seeing her through Roman eyes as an evil and predatory courtesan; nor did Antony fare much better. But it is from Plutarch that he took the description of Cleopatra's first meeting with Antony on her magnificent barge, and it is Plutarch who also shows us some of the more human side of the Queen of Egypt—her dressing as a boy to roam the city streets, for example.

Possibly because of the sheer technical difficulties of the role and the possibility that it was beyond the range of any boy actor who would be playing the women's parts, there is no record of any performance of the play in Shakespeare's own time, nor is there any definite proof that it was played for a long time afterwards. As Speaight says, 'there were certain kinds of scenes which a boy could not decently enact'.

In 1677 Dryden's *All For Love*, which he based on the Shakespeare play, was published and this version swept the board for over a hundred years. In fact, in the seventeenth and early eighteenth centuries, not only was the Dryden play the most popular, it is impossible to disentangle in some cases which play was performed; sometimes theatrical managements put on productions which appear to have been cobbled-up versions of both plays combined.

The first major production appears to have been that of Garrick in 1759. He played Antony, and Mrs Yates, Cleopatra—in a hooped ball gown and a high wig. 'This play,' says a contemporary source, 'tho' new-dress'd and had fine scenes did not seem to give ye audience any great pleasure or draw any Applause.' It folded after six nights, although Garrick had carefully removed any *double entendres*, 'especially among the low folk', in case of offence.

Although it has been said that Mrs Siddons never attempted the Egyptian Queen, she appears to have done so in 1788, playing opposite Kemble in a rather less than accurate version of the text. This also closed very quickly, and an unnamed critic writing in a journal of the day commented merely, 'the part of the Queen is *not* among Mrs Siddons' Triumphs'.

1833 saw another disaster, this time with the actor Macready playing Antony and Mrs Phillips, Cleopatra, who was described as 'totally inadequate'. The play folded after three nights. The first person to draw anything in the nature of rave reviews in the role was Isabella Glyn in a version put on by Samuel Phelps at Sadler's Wells in 1849. She was so successful that she played it again in 1855, and came out of retirement for a repeat performance in 1867. The *Morning Post* critic said of the first production that Mr Phelps's Antony achieved 'well-studied bacchanalian attitudes', and that Miss Glyn's performance of Cleopatra 'is the most superb thing ever witnessed on the modern stage'. This seems hard to believe from the photographs, which show a lady looking almost exactly like Queen Victoria in middle age, wearing a crinoline and with only a marginal reference to anything Egyptian about her.

In 1898 the glamorous Lillie Langtry attempted the part. She is portrayed lolling on a *chaise longue*, but there was not much critical acclaim (although Arthur Symons in a glutinous programme note says, 'to Mrs. Langtry belongs the honour—for it is an honour as well as a credit—for having done more for this incomparable drama than anyone has ever done before'.

But we have to come into the twentieth century before the greater part of the reviews ceased to be devoted to the splendour of the scenery and moved on to an attempt to understand the major roles. Even so, as late as 1912, the *Morning Post* critic could write of Dorothy Green—a famous and successful Cleopatra—'hers was scarcely an overpowering piece of acting, she relied a great deal on rigidity of features, a gazing, as t'were, into space,' although he went on to say that her 'dress shows great taste, skill and completeness of workmanship'.

For the next twenty years it was not a part which added to the stature of many of those, however famous and talented, who attempted it. Edith Evans was praised for 'classical Shakespeare acting' in 1946, and Vivien Leigh was described as 'kittenish' in 1951. It took Dame Peggy Ashcroft in the Stratford production of 1953 to set critics and audience aflame again. Alan Dent wrote of her that 'she manages not only to suggest but to exemplify the royal wench, the most triumphant lady, the ripe gypsy, the serpent by the river Nile, the trull, the boggler, the Egyptian dish, the great fairy, the nightingale, Egypt and, finally, the lass unparalleled'.

It was not acted again at Stratford until 1972, when Janet Suzman took the part splendidly, opposite Richard Johnson's Antony. Barbara Jefford has played the part three times, in Oxford in 1974, Nottingham in 1975 and more recently in 1977 when she took over the role from Dorothy Tutin at the Old Vic who only gave a handful of performances. In 1978 there came the Peter Brook production at Stratford with Glenda Jackson as Cleopatra.

If Cleopatra has made few reputations on the stage, film versions seem to have been even more disastrous. Theda Bara starred in a silent version in 1917, and in 1963 came the Elizabeth Taylor/Richard Burton epic—thankfully not using Shakespeare's words—the most expensive film of its day and which also produced a notorious scandal. In the early 1970s there was an earnest but dull attempt at filming the play, made by Charlton Heston who also played Antony. Hildegard Neil was Cleopatra, and the *Guardian* described it unkindly as 'the Biggest Asp Disaster in the World'.

Looking back through old prints and photographs, no other play can look so curiously dated, or in some cases so ridiculous. It seems, as Janet Suzman says, to lend itself all too well to the Morecambe and Wise send-up. The eighteenth-century ladies played it in panniers, Lillie Langtry as an Edwardian lady. Theda Bara wears a costume apparently made out of a couple of saucepan lids and a skirt like those seen in the television show *Come Dancing*. Early twentieth-century production pictures just look camp. A Russian version in 1962 shows a massive lady looking like a female tank commander, whose huge brassière and massive trousers are hauled together for decency's sake by an enormous expanse of thick cotton-net curtaining.

It is because the part is so difficult to portray visually that past pictures can look so odd. When we look at the text of the play we see, as Robert Speaight reminds us, that Shakespeare very cleverly never describes Cleopatra's physical appearance, 'any more than Homer describes Helen in the *Iliad*; he describes her setting—the cloth of gold pavilion—and her effect upon other people'. Coleridge, not surprisingly in view of his admiration for Helena, does not find Cleopatra attractive. 'The art displayed in the character of Cleopatra is profound in this, especially, that the sense of criminality in her passion is lessened by our insight into its depth and energy at the very moment that we cannot but perceive that the passion itself springs out of the habitual craving of a licentious nature, and that it is supported and reinforced by voluntary stimulus and sought-for associations instead of blossoming out of spontaneous emotion.' 'We do not mistake this feeling of Cleopatra towards Antony for love,' said Edward Dowden, 'but he has been for her (who had known Caesar and Pompey) the supreme sensation.'

Harley Granville-Barker, writing in 1930, said that as Cleopatra was written for a boy, this determined Shakespeare's way of presenting her. A modern dramatist would give us the tragedy of the play's end, 'but can we conceive him leaving Cleopatra without one single scene in which to show the sensual charm which drew Antony to her, and back to her, which is the tragedy's very fount? Yet this is what Shakespeare does, and with excellent reason: a boy could not show it, except objectionably or ridiculously. He does not shirk her sensuality, he stresses it time and again; but he has to find other ways than the one impracticable way of bringing it home to us.'

For Ellen Terry Cleopatra had to be an all-out courtesan. 'Shakespeare has done what no other writer, novelist, dramatist or poet has done—told the truth about the wanton. Yes, Cleopatra is that, and if she is represented as a great woman with a great and sincere passion for Antony, then the part does not hang together.'

A. L. Rowse sees her very fully: 'infinitely various, changing from one iridescent mood to another mercurial and bewitching, ready to rage and storm and beat her attendants. She well knew how to seduce Antony's heart and keep him tethered to her, himself a leading figure in the Roman world—for she was "cunning past man's thought".' For all her femininity, she was also a political type, he continues, who managed to outwit even Octavius Caesar. 'She was an enchantress, almost a sorceress, full of the lore of the East and its credulity, listening to fortune tellers and soothsayers. And yet always, and improbably, she is regal, the descendant of many kings: she does not have to care about dignity.'

She is also, he reminds us, 'the incarnation of sex, more so than any other woman in Shakespeare, and in a different kind'. What he says too is echoed by all the actresses who have recently attempted her. 'When all is said, Cleopatra is the most wonderful woman in Shakespeare. She is the most complex, exotic and compelling to the imagination. It is essential to get her right.'

Getting her right is a formidable task, and what makes it so fascinating is how different actresses see that rightness—sometimes in utterly opposite ways.

For Dame Peggy Ashcroft, who played it opposite Sir Michael Redgrave, 'it remains in my mind so clearly because it is the most exciting role you are ever likely to play. In spite of the enormous challenge it presented, it was certainly one of my happiest experiences—perhaps because of that challenge.

'You can see throughout what you are aiming at—the problem is getting there. With Cleopatra you can never succeed totally because she is so much of everything. You just show some of her. I had a splendid director in Glen Byam Shaw in whom I had great trust and that is absolutely necessary.'

Dame Peggy played Cleopatra 'as the daughter of the Ptolemies, a Greek—pale, with red hair—the Queen of Egypt but *not* an Egyptian. Though she speaks of herself as being "with Phoebus amorous pinches black", I believe that to be an ironical reference to her age—she couples it with "and wrinkled deep in time".

'She was, in fact, in her late thirties. To me her Greek origins were of great importance. I think they bring her closer to our immediate understanding—and her assumption of Eastern splendour and Eastern mystery are part of her armoury of fascinations. Twenty years before I had attempted Shaw's *Cleopatra* and tried to look like Nefertiti—a mistake I think now.

'Because of her famous "infinite variety" how can one define her basic quality? She is brave and cowardly, mean and generous, false yet true, above all passionate and wilful—and devouring. What she wants, she takes and what she wants to do she does. I think of it as Antony's tragedy torn between Rome and the East, between discipline and indulgence. Cleopatra brings about his death and is absolute in her belief that she will join him by killing herself. Really it is the tragedy of Antony, not of Cleopatra. What a fantastic climax that fifth Act is—Cleopatra at her most sublime and yet ready to trick and lie almost to the very end.

'I was appalled and astonished when asked to play her. I thought I was not ready for it and that I could never do it. I was concerned that it was not within my sphere. But I had implicit trust in my director and I found the part takes charge of you. There is no right way of playing Cleopatra—just an infinite number of ways. She is light, she is dark, she is *everything*.'

Janet Suzman, Stratford's next Cleopatra, thinks it theatre's 'most demanding role. It's wonderful to be stretched absolutely to the full. I think one of the main difficulties is a technical one—that of saving yourself enough throughout to carry the long last Act. Although Antony bears the brunt of the major part of the play, there is that last coda and if the balance is as it should be, it becomes the most miraculous thing to act.'

For her one of the play's most important scenes is all too often cut—that between Seleucus and Cleopatra at the end of the play, when Seleucus admits to Octavius Caesar that he has gone through Cleopatra's inventory of her treasure and that it is incomplete. 'I shall always be grateful to Trevor [Trevor Nunn, her husband, who directed her] for leaving that scene in, for it is *very* Cleopatra. She can cheat right at the very end.

'Any actress who says she does not want to do it needs her head examined. It's something you cannot miss in the landscape of drama. If you think about the descriptions of her then you couldn't possibly do it but Shakespeare is so brilliant because he only allows himself hints of what he says about her to actually appear in the scenes on the stage.

'I find it hard to think he wrote it for a boy. I think he must have written it for a man, perhaps a kind of Shakespearean Danny La Rue—there must have been some kind of prima donna in his company playing women's parts and men are notoriously good at it. It could never have been acted by a boy—Portia, Rosalind, Viola, yes—they could be breathtaking played by a stripling, a clear young spirit, but not Cleopatra.

'Shakespeare gets her exactly right. "Let him forever go, let him stay"—this is Cleopatra. She has miraculous extremes of temperament and of desire. It is breathless trying to keep up with her if you look at her in natural terms. He has done no more and no less than write about a large spirit. It is exhilarating in its sheer womanliness and femininity. Shakespeare always loved that aspect of women, that true womanliness. When she is most shameless, that is when one is most drawn to her. Perhaps it is the dynamic element in her which is the most elusive thing to achieve and it is ever-present. She reminds you all the time that she is the Queen of Egypt and that undertow of her regality, her inherited power, her dynastic blood, is constant throughout the play. Yet she can turn and flirt when her realm is at stake.

'Perhaps there was something of Queen Elizabeth in her—a certain fibrous quality—but he gave her the freedom only a foreign Queen could have. Even Elizabeth had to refer to Cecil, she had to refer to nobody. I never felt that she was a European even though she is historically a Ptolemy. She is the Queen of Egypt, darkly foreign, where everything else is pale. She exudes the exotic.

'The language itself is almost too lush. Fortunately she gets a good many half lines when she says very pointed, wicked or uneven things yet her poetry when it is high is of the highest.

'She lived in a true golden age. It is a part too mighty to get all of—each Cleopatra will be better at certain aspects—the cruel, the childish, regal, funny, wicked, sexy; but an actor attempting it has at least to try to encompass them all. And throughout is the difference between Rome and Egypt—the exotic, relaxed indulgence of Egypt and its effect on the martial discipline of Rome. I think that was an aspect we got over very well in our production.

'But the eternal teasing question, the sand in the oyster, and the chiefest stroke of Shakespeare's genius is just *how* much in love with Anthony she really was. It is the eternal ambiguity, that question of their love. That's why it is so difficult to play Antony. He has to be absolutely in thrall—she leads and he follows—even from the battlefield. There is not one single time when she is not Cleopatra and her very inconstancy is the realest thing about her.'

Barbara Jefford has no doubts at all about Cleopatra's love for Antony. 'That first scene between them is crucial. It has everything of their relationship in it except the tragedy. You have to establish right away the strength of their feelings—these disgraceful carryings-on. It's got to be passionate, full of feeling, even torrid. There must be incense, hangings, cushions on the floor. When we played it at the Old Vic in 1978, Antony and Cleopatra exchanged robes with each other while they were speaking—something they did in real life, to more closely identify with each other. "If this be love indeed, tell me how much," she says, and it must, indeed, be love.

'The hardest thing is the emphasis on her changeability which lasts throughout the play and goes on through the whole gamut in the scene where Antony says although his wife is dead he will still leave Egypt for Rome. It is the difficulty of not making Cleopatra tricky or facile. You can't play her just sexy, kittenish or cruel, she's too womanly—you've got to try and be everything. I can't imagine what kind of boy played it at the time it was written— perhaps no one ever did and perhaps that is why it was hardly ever played.

'It is the one part you cannot play without experience or a run up to it. It confers tremendous benefits on an actress because you have to have such courage to attempt it, the almost impossibility of getting all those changes.'

Like Janet Suzman, Barbara Jefford sees Cleopatra as dark and foreign, 'not a red-haired Ptolemy. She talks about "Phoebus' amorous pinches", she was dark and sunburnt, a gypsy. She uses her wiles as nobody does, from minute to minute and pretends right up to the very end. There is this double feeling even when she is intending to do away with herself and she's half dead with grief. It's extraordinary. All that Shakespeare says of her must have been true—that truly terrible games' playing, the ability to be charming and then turn round and give you bloody teeth. She's despotic, a frightening woman and you must never feel that danger is far away. Frank Hauser, who directed me first, said 'If you want to cross the stage just go—people will melt away in front of you, they would have done . . .'

'However tremendous her grief she never loses her head. She makes a good death, something necessary in her time. She achieves it, Antony bungles his. I'm lucky to have played it each time with my husband [John Turner] although he wasn't my husband the first time. There's got to be real sympathy between them in real life, if not a grand passion. I'd love to do it again while I feel physically able—I feel I could get nearer to it now.'

Glenda Jackson was the most recent Stratford Cleopatra in Peter Brook's 1978 production. There was no magnificence or splendour about Brook's vision of Egypt, and Antony and Cleopatra played out their tragedy on a stark stage as if in an ante-room, out of the limelight.

'It is', she said, 'if not the most difficult part to play then the most difficult in the classical canon. Probably the hardest thing is to make the words do the work, that and her speed. I am naturally slow and it is the speed with which she works internally that I found difficult to attune to, those changes and shifts of mood which are quite genuine. They are not arbitrary—something put in for the external eye—they are her essential nature.

'As to her attractiveness, if you try and play it mainly on that level then you are on a hiding to nothing. You always suffer anyway from what is considered to be attractive and desirable in a woman—it is always far less, of course, than that demanded of a man put at its lowest level.

'The text is so dense, it's such an extraordinary play. The more work you do on it the more you discover how much there is to be done. When I first looked at the part and read one of those texts with commentaries and scene changes and lists of characters at the head of each page, it seemed a hopeless muddle. I just had to stop and read through the text without checking to see who was who or what was what, just like a long letter or a poem. You can pick out any two lines anywhere and it is monumental.

'But I found that although it is always described as an "epic" play, it's not that at all. They are epic people but they are making human decisions, suffering human emotions. They are acting out their lives in private rooms and are most intimate, in a sense. You get this tremendous sense of millions of people outside, pressing against doors and windows, whose lives depend on those extraordinary beings and Shakespeare does it all in words.

'He's so specific, so varied in his understanding and sensitivity to everything. He had to have written those plays—nobody else could have sustained them. He writes with a unique rightness about Antony and Cleopatra. Their whole lives and the way they behave is intensely human, it is—above all—a human tragedy and it is human emotions, if of a large size, that move them. There was nothing of hatred and contempt for his characters in Shakespeare—unlike all too many modern writers. He had enormous personal involvement and infinite compassion. Oh, where is he now, one wonders?

'As to Cleopatra—you just get sudden little glimpses of her as you work. The sheer impossibility of making yourself so extraordinary a being is so huge that you cannot ask yourself if she is astute, cruel, kind—it's pointless. You have to just go in there and work. I have this feeling that she is much simpler—and therefore much more dangerous—than we can actually grasp.'

Janet Suzman sums up Cleopatra, the eternal tease. 'Of course one would like to do her once more—to cross those shimmering distances—but perhaps you can only walk those particular streets once. Cleopatra? In the midst of truth, she lies in her teeth, in the midst of anger, she cries unashamedly, in the midst of high seriousness, she can crack a joke. And in the midst of dying she has time to stop and consider what dying is like.'

'This rough magic . . .'

If *Henry VIII* was Shakespeare's last play, then it is likely to have been a collaborative effort. His last full work, and a summation of his life's work, was *The Tempest*, and it is surely not sentimental or whimsical to see the laying down of that work in Prospero's farewell:

> Our revels now are ended. These our actors
> As I foretold you, were all spirits, and
> Are melted into air, into thin air:
> And like the baseless fabric of this vision,
> The cloud-capp'd towers, the gorgeous palaces,
> The solemn temples, the great globe itself,
> Yea, all which it inherit, shall dissolve,
> And, like this insubstantial pageant faded,
> Leave not a wrack behind. We are such stuff
> As dreams are made on; and our little life
> Is rounded with a sleep . . .

Did he think his creations would dissolve into thin air? We do not know, but one imagines he did not. Few other writers have produced such an array of fully rounded human beings, totally believable in their virtues and failings.

Dr Henry Yellowlees, in the lecture already quoted on medical matters in Shakespeare's plays, ended: 'So comes Shakespeare's greatest miracle, that we regard people who never existed outside his imagination as real and living acquaintances of our own, who we shall know at once if we met them on leaving this hall. As I have been speaking, the miracle has once more been at work, on me at least. I can see Sir Toby at the door of the *Duck*, hoping to find someone who will stand him a drink. Dogberry and Juliet's nurse are inside it, exchanging verbose reminiscences and pointless anecdotes . . . and there, coming down the street, is dear old Peter Quince with a worried look on his face and carrying an enormous basket of stage properties.'

It is their reality which fascinates. When we look back on the range of Shakespeare's women we see them progress from the monstrous Margaret of Anjou and the unsympathetic version of Joan of Arc, through the shrews of the very early comedies, to the golden girls, the patient suffering women and shining innocence of Miranda. It is not necessary to know the details of Shakespeare's relationships with women to see that his vision and feelings towards them deepened and altered as time went by.

Cressida was a throwback again to a wanton, but even in the two great female roles—Lady Macbeth and Cleopatra—although both have frightening aspects and tremendous complexity neither have the feeling of inhumanity with which Shakespeare invested Tamora and Margaret. Everything seems to point to a tremendous emotional upheaval in the early 1590s, and during that period the Dark Lady of the Sonnets—whoever she was—had a bitter and profound effect on his view of women, towards whom he truly felt the expense of spirit in a waste of shame.

Although some commentators see only Rosaline as bearing a resemblance to his dark mistress, Ivor Brown saw traces of her in many more of the plays, beginning with Tamora in *Titus Andronicus*, through Rosaline and Beatrice and Cressida right up to Cleopatra.

'In *Antony and Cleopatra*', he says, 'Shakespeare was to paint her for the last time and almost to forgive her. Why this change of mind? Because, I believe, she was by that time dead.' Quoting the lines on 'a lass unparallel'd', he says, 'the brief, affectionate "lass", the weighty rolling "unparallel'd"—they are typical of Shakespeare's magic. They are also a proclamation of pardon, a statement of forgiveness as well as of farewell to the wanton Cleopatra certainly and, as I think, to another also, the poet's own love of ecstasy and despair. This, at least, is beyond dispute: that if we owe some of the sonnets and all of *Antony and Cleopatra* to a Lady

Anon, a Tudor-Jacobean beauty of her day, then our debt to that unnamed, elusive creature outranges calculation.'

A. L. Rowse says of Shakespeare's portrayal of women: 'Shakespeare is the sexiest great writer in the language. . . . His mind, quite naturally and effortlessly, dripped sex at every pore. . . . It is a most important element in his mind and make up, the salty element that acts along with the rest as a preservative of his work. As Partridge says, Shakespeare not only very much enjoyed sex but took a lively, very curious interest in it: "He was no more an instinctive sensualist, but an intellectual voluptuary and a thinker keenly, shrewdly, penetratingly, probing into sex, its mysteries, its mechanism, its exercise and its expertise and its influence on life and character." There is not only plain bawdy which we can all recognize but there is the continual fountainplay of innuendo which not all nice minds can grasp at first sight. . . . His fixation on women, his fascinated adoration of them, his sympathetic understanding of all varieties of feminine nature, his unquenched ardour, his undying love of women—all this is utterly obvious from beginning to end of his work.

'Hence the most marvellous gallery of female characters in literature.'

The first women to appear on a public stage were Mrs Hughes, playing Desdemona, and Mrs Rutter, Emilia, in a presentation of *Othello* by Thomas Killigrew at Drury Lane in 1660. From then on the Shakespeare women have been the plums towards which the great actresses have worked. Acting is such an ephemeral business. Nowadays we can hand on film of how the roles were portrayed in the twentieth century but before that we have to rely on memories of great performances. Mrs Siddons, we are told, made audiences faint with the ferocity of her outbursts as Cleopatra, yet, as Mrs Jameson writes, she could also move them to easy tears as Ophelia.

There is no doubt that those who have played the roles appreciate what Shakespeare gave them. Dame Ellen Terry says: 'Wonderful women—have you ever thought how much we all, and women especially, owe to Shakespeare for his vindication of women in the fearless, high-spirited, resolute and intelligent heroines? Don't believe the anti-feminists when they tell you, as I was once told, that Shakespeare had to endow his women with virile qualities because in his theatre they were always impersonated by men. This may account for the frequency with which they masquerade as boys but I am convinced that it had little influence on Shakespeare's studies of women.'

Lilian Bayliss of the Old Vic, more noted for tactlessness in comment than anything else ('quite nice, dear, if a trifle suburban', she told an aspiring Portia), waxed lyrical over Shakespeare's heroines. 'In spite, or perhaps because of, the fact that the parts were written to be played by boy actors, they are always essentially feminine because they are eminently practical. "Do you not know I am a woman?", says Rosalind, "when I think I must speak." But they not only speak, but act to the purpose. Romeo, banished, flings himself on the ground with his own tears made drunk, Juliet devises ways and means of escape from the meshes of fate. Macbeth and Hamlet postpone and vacillate and torture themselves with doubts and regrets. Lady Macbeth, having made up her mind, never hesitates and never looks back. What is done is done. It is this matter of fact view, combined with their tenderness and inherent modesty, notwithstanding their speech and action, which keeps them before us as true women even when disguised in doublet and hose.

'Compared with the heroines of most of his contemporaries, and of the eighteenth-century dramatists or Victorian novelists, Shakespeare's heroines are extraordinarily modern and this, no doubt, explains the hold they have over the audience today.'

Writing in the thirties, in an introduction to a booklet on a Shakespeare series designed for BBC radio, Dame Edith Evans said: 'From the point of view of an actress, the Shakespeare women are most satisfactory people, for when portrayed they actually seem to feed the artist even when she is giving out the most of herself in the performance of her part. They are so true; their nobility, beauty, tenderness, loveliness, lightheartedness, subtlety, provocativeness, passion, vengefulness, worthlessness, stupidity and a hundred more qualities are so entirely right from the feminine point of view that they provide a field the most ambitious artist can scarcely hope to cover. They are a feast at which one is fed while serving.'

Dame Peggy Ashcroft speaks of the fact that there will never, happily, be a definitive way of playing a role, only an infinite number of ways. Jane Lapotaire says that in 'all the plays he pays you back a thousandfold what you put in. Scales continually fall off your eyes and from your ears all the time you are working on them.'

Judi Dench says that *Twelfth Night* alone shows you every facet of human love. For however thoroughly or constantly scholars analyse them, and however useful it is for actresses to know how they are constructed and how the verse works, the plays are, after all, meant to be offered in performance, not pored over in the quietness of the study.

The last words I will leave with Janet Suzman. 'What makes the roles so wonderful? I believe that it is partly because neither the Elizabethans nor Jacobeans were in the least frightened of women. They wrote about them with such perception and such passionate accuracy that I would guess their relationships with women were healthy and unthreatened. Just look for example at Donne's love poetry! I suspect it may be because they had been ruled by a woman for so long that it became allowable for women to be considered astonishing and remarkable. The quality of Queen Elizabeth's mind was both these things. There is never anything in the least patronizing about Shakespeare's attitude to the intelligence of his women.

'And he had so much understanding of their weaknesses. Ophelia, Juliet; only a very great poet could recall how blazingly malleable one is when one is young; the appalling worries; the despair; how passionately one feels about every little thing, how vulnerable. Or Beatrice, all wickedness and cracking wit outside, but inside all hidden woman's heart, melting with fervour. Oh, I could go on and on. . . . Shakespeare provides an actress with such a rich diet that it is sometimes difficult to turn to other things as hungrily. No doubt at all; he loved women; in an Englishman, dare I say it, a rare weakness, and consequently infinitely treasurable.'

Select Bibliography

N.B. *The body of works on all aspects of Shakespeare is enormous. Below is a selection of those that I found most useful.*

A. C. Bradley, *Shakespearean Tragedy* (London 1904)

Ivor Brown, *Shakespeare* (London 1949)
  Shakespeare and the Actors (London 1970)

Geoffrey Bullough (ed.), *Narrative and Dramatic Sources of Shakespeare*
  8 Vols. London 1957–75

Thomas Campbell, *Life of Mrs Siddons*, London 1834–9

E. K. Chambers, *William Shakespeare* (London and N.Y. 1930)
  The Elizabethan Stage 4 Vols. (London 1923)
  Shakespearean Gleanings (London and N.Y. 1944)

Neville Coghill, *Shakespeare's Professional Skills* (London 1964)

S. T. Coleridge, *Essays and Lectures on Shakespeare* (London 1849)
  Shakespearean Criticism (London 1849. ed. reprint 1960)

J. Dover Wilson *The Essential Shakespeare* (London and N.Y. 1960)
  What Happens in 'Hamlet' (Cambridge 1935)

L. Fiedler, *The Stranger in Shakespeare* (N.Y. 1960, London 1973)

J. Garrett (ed.), *More Talking of Shakespeare* (London 1959)

George Geckle (ed.), *20th Century Interpretations of Measure for Measure*
  (N.Y. 1970)

H. Granville-Barker, *Prefaces to Shakespeare: Four Series* (London
  1927–46)

F. E. Halliday, *The Life of Shakespeare* (London 1961)
  Shakespeare and his Critics (London 1949)

W. Hazlitt, *Characters of Shakespeare's Plays* (London 1817)

L. Hotson, *The First Night of 'Twelfth Night'* (London 1954)
  Shakespeare versus Shallow (London 1931)

H. Hunt, *Old Vic Prefaces: Shakespeare and Producer* (London 1954)

A. Jameson, *Shakespeare's Heroines* (London 1832; 1833)

L. C. Knights, *An Approach to Hamlet* (London 1960)
  Some Shakespearean Themes (London 1959)
  Explorations (London 1946)

J. Kott, *Shakespeare Our Contemporary* (London 1965; rev. 1967)

Kenneth Muir and Sean O'Loughlin, *The Voyage to Illyria* (London
  1937)

K. Muir and P. Edwards (eds) *Aspects of Macbeth* (Cambridge 1976)
Oxford Companion to the Theatre, third edition (Oxford 1967)
P. Quennell, *Shakespeare, the Poet and His Background* (London 1963)
A. L. Rowse, *William Shakespeare* (London and N.Y. 1963)
   The Case Book of Simon Forman (London 1974)
R. Speaight, *Shakespeare, The Man and his Achievement* (London 1977)
E. Terry, *Four Lectures on Shakespeare* (London 1932)
D. Traversi, *An Approach to Shakespeare* (London 1957)
   Shakespeare: The Roman Plays (London 1963)
J. Wain, *The Living World of Shakespeare* (London 1964)
   A Selection of Critical Essays (London 1968)
E. Wilson (edited) *Shaw on Shakespeare* (London 1962)

I used the Oxford University Press complete works, and for working on individual texts the new *Arden Editions of Shakespeare*, published by Methuen, of which the following introductions were particularly helpful:

Agnes Latham on *As You Like It*
Kenneth Muir on *Macbeth*
J. W. Lever on *Measure for Measure*
J. R. Brown on *Merchant of Venice*
M. R. Ridley on *Othello*
J. M. Lothian and T. W. Craik on *Twelfth Night*
F Kermode on *The Tempest*

Also very useful were the programme notes by Anne Barton, written for a variety of Royal Shakespeare Company productions at Stratford.

Index

N.B. *Shakespeare's plays are listed under his name. However, if a reference is to a character—e.g. Macbeth—who gives his name to a play, it will be found in the correct alphabetical position.*